Monologues
and Duologues
for the Drama Studio

JEFFREY GRENFELL-HILL

SilverWood

Published in 2022 by SilverWood Books

SilverWood Books Ltd
14 Small Street, Bristol, BS1 1DE, United Kingdom
www.silverwoodbooks.co.uk

Copyright © Jeffrey Grenfell-Hill 2022

ISBN 978-1-80042-219-3 (paperback)

British Library Cataloguing in Publication Data
A CIP catalogue record for this book is
available from the British Library

Page design and typesetting by SilverWood Books

This book is dedicated to my dear wife, Muriel Anne,
whose constant support helps me find the space to be creative.

Contents

Introduction

Scriptwriting for the younger actor presents many challenges. The principal challenge is finding themes for the actor to explore and bring to life. Giving life and credibility to the written word is part of an actor's craft. I hope that I have created scenes in which the actor can enter into a world of exploration and a deeper understanding of dramatic possibilities.

Teaching drama to young actors opens up many opportunities for vocabulary development, imaginative exploration and empathy. In these scenes, I have tried to create a sense of involvement with the unseen – with an unseen friend or in the character's significant involvement in the world around them. The monologues are not mono-thoughts; rather, they are a series of emotive reactions to a multiplicity of thought patterns. An actor should be aware that a full stop means the end of a thought – what comes in the next sentence is a new thought. Full stop patterns are an important framework on which to hang one's understanding of emotional levels within a script. Ignoring the value of a full stop can result in over-pacing a scene and neglecting to show that thought precedes the spoken links to how the character is feeling – think it first and then reveal it.

Acting is more than merely learning lines. It is an empathetic exploration of each moment and the character's involvement in those moments. An actor's craft is to become someone else in a spontaneous and truthful portrayal.

In the following scenes, I offer drama scope for cross-curricular links. I begin with scenes inspired by a number of William Shakespeare's plays. From my previous collection of monologues, *Monologues and Duologues for the Young Actor*, the monologue *Cobweb with the Indian Boy* has proved a popular choice at drama festivals, and my scene *In Portia's Kitchen* has been chosen from the LAMDA acting syllabus by countless exam candidates. This encouraged me to write the six new monologues included in this collection and a duologue set backstage at The Globe.

Given that World War I is included in most school curricula, I have included scenes from my two-act play *Blighty 1914–1918* to provide actors with more opportunities to explore different elements of that war. These include opportunities for Voluntary Aid Detachments (VADs) and soldiers to reveal different attitudes to war in the trenches. These scenes also complement the history curriculum by providing students with the tools to open their minds to how people related differently to warfare.

Actors can find out about the different attitudes soldiers held during the fighting.

It is also my intention to encourage actors to use mime as a supportive element within characterisation. Some scenes allow for more extensive mime sequences than others. Teachers can encourage actors to fully explore this adjunct to portrayal as it is one of the building blocks of insightful projection of the text.

I hope these scenes will be enjoyed by countless actors who will wrap themselves in a mantle that is other than themselves.

Jeffrey Grenfell-Hill, Angel Cottage

A guide to help you find your character

As an actor learning the skills of your craft (ie finding the mindset of the character you are to perform) the following tools will be of help:

» Highlight any words or phrases when you are unsure about the intention or meaning. If necessary, conduct some research to extend your knowledge.

» As an actor, always be proactive in asking questions about your role:

» What is the purpose of the scene?

» Are there different objectives?

» Are different moods being generated?

It may be a useful exercise to create spider diagrams to help you to think in greater detail about key features of purpose/objective/mood. At a glance, you can identify your journey.

Your craft skills are to create a character who is believable.

• How would you describe your character?

• As you portray your character's emotions, which ones do you need to highlight or concentrate on?

Learn to constantly update and develop the tools of modulation that you command. These factors are in your vocal toolbox. Write a note beside each one:

• Pace
• Pitch
• Pause
• Tone
• How would you describe your character's physicality?
• If you are preparing a duologue scene, consider whether the two characters have different personalities.
• Duologue actors could devise questions to ask each other during

a 'hot seat' session. The more you can discover about each other the better your performance will be.

- Take a phrase and imagine what your character is feeling. You may reveal a number of different feelings.
- As an actor, keep in mind the intentions of the scriptwriter and how you will convey this to the audience through a meaningful characterisation.
- Remember, as an actor, it is your job to create a believable line of dramatic involvement, which builds up to a memorable climax.
- Visual impact can be an important element of a performance. Make and annotate a sketch of what your character would look like. Imagine you are a theatrical costume designer and choose your materials (cotton, silk, chiffon, tweed, cambric, nylon, wool blend, canvas, etc).

Use these guidelines to build and get to know your character, to understand their motivation and intention, and to inhabit your scene and bring it to life.

Good luck on your journey!

The Stepsisters' Plan

Cinderella's stepsisters, Petronella and Citronella, have been watching the prince put the glass slipper onto their stepsister's foot. They are outraged and disappointed by this turn of events. Eventually, they work out a plan.

PETRONELLA: (*Angrily*) Did you see how Cinders had to push an' push to get her foot into that glass slipper? It wasn't easy…

CITRONELLA: And now the prince has gone off thinking he's got the right girl.

PETRONELLA: (*Calling out*) Hey, Cinders! The prince will soon discover how bad-natured you are…

CITRONELLA: He'll find out about your temper tantrums…

PETRONELLA: And how vain you are.

CITRONELLA: Not sweet-natured like me…

PETRONELLA: And me!

TOGETHER: We are both sweeter tempered than you. (*Pointing angrily at Cinderella and poking out their tongues*)

PETRONELLA: What? You're going off to buy some better clothes?

CITRONELLA: What? The prince has given you his platinum debit card… so you're off to Harrods? (*Calling out*) Well, good riddance!

PETRONELLA: (*Calling after her*) You'll soon get your comeuppance when the king and queen discover you're only a *baroness*!

CITRONELLA: Oh! Come on, Petti. Let's go off to our boudoir and think this through…(*They cross the stage and mime going into another room. Chairs are placed before their dressing table upon which they have cosmetics.*)

PETRONELLA: (*Falling into a chair*) This turn out has really put me down in the dumps.

CITRONELLA: Well, that's not new. You're always in the dumps. (*Sitting*)

PETRONELLA: No one can say that you're always a bundle of laughs either,

Citti. Your mouth is always turned down like this! (*She makes an ugly face at her sister*)

CITRONELLA: That's a hundred times better than your permanently ugly face being forced on me.

PETRONELLA: Oh, shut up!

CITRONELLA: Shut up yourself, big mouth!

(*They fold their arms with displeasure and sit sulking*)

PETRONELLA: Hey! We could work this to our advantage. (*She snaps her fingers*) Old Cinders will have a big wedding…

CITRONELLA: And Mama will buy us new clothes.

PETRONELLA: The best designers.

CITRONELLA: Handbags and shoes to match.

PETRONELLA: And jewels. We'll have to have jewels.

CITRONELLA: It's emeralds for me to match my gorgeous green eyes…

PETRONELLA: Who are you kidding? For me, it's sapphires to match my exquisitely blue eyes.

CITRONELLA: You've gotta be blind!

PETRONELLA: There will be hundreds of guests at the wedding.

CITRONELLA: Handsome men everywhere.

PETRONELLA: We'll find husbands, Citti. Rich husbands.

CITRONELLA: As sisters of Princess Charming, we'll be the best catches of the season.

PETRONELLA: Yes! And when Cinders is living at the palace, we'll get to go to all of the balls there…

CITRONELLA: Balls with scrumptious food to eat…

PETRONELLA: And men.

CITRONELLA: And Champagne…

PETRONELLA: And men.

CITRONELLA: Life could start being really exciting. Little stepsister could be our ticket to life's luxuries.

PETRONELLA: And men.

CITRONELLA: For heaven's sake, Petti, you've got a one-track mind. Men on the brain, I call it…

PETRONELLA: (*Suddenly gripping her sister's arm*) Hey, Citti, we've got to start being 'nice' to Cinders.

CITRONELLA: Yes! Extra 'nice'.

PETRONELLA: Like smiling at her.

CITRONELLA: Smiling!

PETRONELLA: And paying her compliments.

CITRONELLA: This is like breaking the habit of a lifetime!

PETRONELLA: It'll be worth it. It's that or exclusion.

CITRONELLA: Exclusion? What do you mean?

PETRONELLA: Are you dim-witted or something?

CITRONELLA: Not as dim as you. Don't call me dim-witted.

PETRONELLA: Well, you are! Don't you realise that old Cinders could decide *not* to invite us to the balls.

CITRONELLA: Ah! Exclude us from the party scene. Yes! I see your point now, Petti.

PETRONELLA: She could block us out…

CITRONELLA: Cast us aside…

PETRONELLA: Ignore us…

CITRONELLA: Tell the prince we're 'undesirables'.

PETRONELLA: Imagine, Citti. Social death!
(*They both gasp. Stunned. They sit in silence for a moment contemplating this fate.*)

CITRONELLA: Right! Citti, put your face on. (*She picks up a lipstick from her dressing table*) And try to make yourself as pretty as me…

PETRONELLA: (*Putting on her lipstick and powder*) Your prettiness is all powder and paint. My face just needs a light touch-up…

CITRONELLA: You never could face the truth… (*They finish their make-up and stand*)

PETRONELLA: Now it's off to Harrods to find Cinders and be super nice to her.

CITRONELLA: Be as nice as pie.

Together: This is a mega charm offensive. (*They smile brilliantly*) Charm personified…
(*They pick up their designer handbags, join arms and go off*)

Fed Up

This scene takes place in the Grand High Witch's Training Academy for Junior Witches where Justina is attending classes, but is not very successful. She has failed her Potions Test and has been told that she must repeat the test and pass it if she is to move up to the next class. She must take the test in front of her classmates, something she is not happy about. (Keep in mind that she has an eyeline that suggests she is speaking directly to a group of classmates seated in an arc before her)

JUSTINA: (*Really cross*) I'm fed up! You can't imagine how fed up I really am. (*She turns to one of the other girls*) It's all right for you, Agatha, you like being a witch… I suppose it's because you always get top marks in the potion-mixing classes… OK… OK…so you're "from a long line of witches dating back to King James I who hanged your umpteenth great grandmother for putting a spell on all the village cows"… (*Sighing deeply*) We've heard it all before…boring…some of us are only third generation witches, like me… OK… OK, so it's in your genes… I suppose I am a newcomer to all this jokery-pokery. (*Suddenly grows alarmed*) Oh! Forget I said that, Agatha. You won't tell the Grand High Witch I said that, will you… please…if she finds out, she'll squiggle-squash me out with a wave of her mega mighty wand. I'll end up as a squiff of smoke…it just came out from nowhere… (*Recovers herself*) Right…deep breath… the GHW has said I have to do this spell again… AND GET IT RIGHT before I get to pass up to the next grade… OK… OK… (*Turns to Agatha in annoyance*) Yes! Agatha…everyone knows I waved my wand and…ended up with "two grey mice instead of six white doves"…you don't need to broadcast it to all the girls, do you? Now everybody, give me some space… Agatha, will you stop breathing down my neck!…it's an invasion of my space and

I need arm-space to wave my wand around... Arabella, hand me the Witches School Ready Mix Potion Plus sachet...right...all I have to do is get my chant right. (*She waves her arms*)

> Mega mix and aim to fix
> A recipe that gives us six
> Dovey-doves and more dovey-doves

(*She waves her wand around*)

> Zoom-Zam Zoom-Zam – voila!

Gosh! I've done it girls...six white doves...it's a triumph!
So, Agatha, I'll be moving up with you. Isn't that great? Oh! Come on, girls, we've got to catch those doves and put them back before they get to that open window...come on Agatha, lend a hand... don't just sit there, grab a dove!

Backstage at The Globe, 1603

This scene of two apprenticed boy actors at The Globe is set in 1603. Plague is raging in London and the theatres have been closed to prevent the spread of infection. These young actors, both of whom play women, are packing up their costumes and props ready to leave for the country mansion of the Earl of Pembroke. The scene involves mimed sequences during which the actors take costumes off rails and props off tables to pack into travelling baskets. The old queen has died and there is a Scottish king, James I.

DIGGORY: Our passage through the countryside will be made easier now that we wear the king's livery. (*He takes a gown from the rail*) No one will call us vagrants.

TOM: (*Taking the gown*) This outbreak of plague* must be serious if the king goes into the country to stay with my Lord of Pembroke. (*He folds the gown into the chest*)
(*Continue with talking, folding and placing the garments and props into the imagined baskets as the dialogue continues. It can be done at a pace that feels right for the actors.*)

DIGGORY: They say the countess has gone to prepare Wilton for the king's visit.

TOM: I hope that their mansion house is big enough for the king and all his court.

DIGGORY: It'll cost the earl more than a shilling or two to feed that lot.

TOM: (*Holding up a cushion*) Shall we take all these penny cushions the nobility sit on?

DIGGORY: (*Laughing*) No! They will have stools and cushions aplenty at Wilton.

TOM: And there won't be any stinkards** at our play.

DIGGORY: There are some lords who don't smell much better than the stinkards!

(*They laugh, grimace and wave their hands under their noses*)

TOM: I am looking forward to no bear-baiting on the other side of the wall.

DIGGORY: And the howling of the dogs in the bear garden.

TOM: All that teasing of bears distracts me from my lines.

DIGGORY: Your Portia lacked conviction last time I played Nerissa.

TOM: The roaring of the bears, the howling of the dogs and the cheering of the people made me forget my lines.

DIGGORY: Well, it won't be like that in Wilton.

TOM: No! I know that! But we won't be there forever. When we have performed before the king and the nobility, we shall go on tour...

DIGGORY: I know what you mean. It will be inn yards and market places.

TOM: And market day can be as noisy as bear-baiting.

DIGGORY: And there's always some cow giving a tremendous moo just as I tell Romeo how much I love him in iambic pentameters.

(*They both move around like cows mooing*)

TOM: And sheep baaing.

DIGGORY: When I am Portia talking to Lord Bassanio.

(*They both move around like sheep baaing*)

TOM: But market day brings in the crowds.

DIGGORY: And pays our wages.

TOM: Oh well, life's like that – full of challenges.

DIGGORY: (*Going and picking up a manuscript from a table*) And we have a new challenge. Our scribe has given me a fair copy of a new play by Mr Shakespeare which we are to perfect.

TOM: Are we to prepare it for the king?

DIGGORY: It is set in Denmark.

TOM: Our queen is from Denmark.

DIGGORY: And we are to start rehearsals again.

TOM: What parts are there for us? I want to be young and beautiful.

DIGGORY: There is a queen and a distressed maiden.

TOM: Are they beautiful?

DIGGORY: Beauty is not the principal factor of this play; it is honour.

TOM: If the queen is fat and plain, Mr Burbage can play her to perfection.

DIGGORY: (*Shocked*) Tom! Mr Burbage never plays women. He has got himself prepared to play the leading role: Hamlet.

Tom: And is the leading role for a fat man with a plain face?

Diggory: You are too harsh on Mr Burbage.

Tom: He is far too pompous and loves himself greatly.

Diggory: The people like him. Indeed, admire him.

Tom: Be that as it may. When I played the Lady Anne to his Richard III, he never complimented me once, although others did, and did it heartily, I can tell you.

Diggory: Well, I'm good at queens. (*He puts down the manuscript*)

Tom: And I'm good at young maidens.

Diggory: Come on. We'd better get a move on.

(*They hurry to complete the packing*)

Tom: Who knows when London will be safe again?

Diggory: We are lucky to be going to Wiltshire with the court...

*The 1603 plague outbreak in London killed 38,000 people.

**A slang word to describe the groundlings who paid a penny to stand and watch the play. Seven hundred people could be crammed into the open yard, their smell creating 'a big stink'.

Portia's Serving Maid, Belmont

Emelia is in her mistress's closet, getting ready the clothes she will wear for Bassanio's visit to Belmont. She stands before a cassone (a chest), taking out and spreading garments on various chairs for display. When not concentrating on the garments, she confidentially addresses the audience.

EMELIA: Our Lady Portia is so excited, you cannot imagine…much more so than when those other suitors appeared…we all had a laugh at them…well, behind their backs, as none of us wants to be whipped for impertinence…our steward is a hard master from Vicenza… (*She spreads a gown out on a chair*) Our Lady likes scarlet…she wore this when that Count of Paris came, all decked out in Paris fashions, and mincing along with a big lace handkerchief in his right hand… (*She demonstrates mincing*) and speaking all that click-cluck French none of us could understand… (*She goes back to the cassone*) Ah! Look at this… (*She mimes taking out another gown*) the blue of the skies, the blue of the Blessed Virgin Mary, our Lady looks lovely in this…she wore it when the German came…now what a sight he was with a big feathered cap all droopy around his ears…a bit grubby and speaking gobbledegook and ya-ya and with his big feet and big belly, he lumbered around these caskets unable to make his mind up…then choosing the wrong one…thank all the saints in heaven. (*She crosses herself*) The sweetest smelling one and definitely the most handsome was that Prince of Morocco…now he was a charmer, all silks and satins and fine jewels in his ears and on his fingers and an amazing diamond pendant around his neck…now he was a sight to behold…a rich prince worthy of our Lady. But he too chose the wrong casket. I suppose we were all relieved because we might have all been carted off to Morocco to serve our Lady in his palace and none of us want to leave Venice or Belmont. So now it's Lord Bassanio's turn…our

Lady has met him before in Venice…and upon consideration, he is handsomer than the Moroccan and, of course, Venetian…we all know she has set her cap on having him as husband…she has told the musicians to sing a special song she has composed…and this is to be sung as he looks at the caskets…if he listens attentively, he'll get the message and choose the right one…it's a bit underhand…isn't it? But when a woman fancies a particular man, she has to have him, you know…and our Lady fancies the Lord Bassanio like crazy. (*She pulls out the last gown*) Aha! Now this is the one I think she'll choose, the white trimmed with gold to match her hair…she'll be a stunner in this…let's all hope he'll get it right. (*She spreads the gown out*) You know how some men don't listen. (*She hears Portia approaching*) Oh! Here my Lady comes. (*Portia enters, Emelia curtseys*) Yes, my Lady, the gowns are ready for you to inspect. (*She gestures towards them*) And your jewels too…

Preparations at Belmont

In this scene, Portia's servants are looking for two of the caskets, which will be put in place upstairs for the suitors to examine. The servant in charge must indicate the unseen servant who will help unlock the storerooms and locate the caskets. There are opportunities for mime sequences and eyeline engagement with the other servant.

SERVANT: Oh! There's such a commotion. The cooks are all busy making preparations for my Lady Portia's suitors to appear. They say there's even a prince from some foreign country. (*Turning to the other servant*) Do you know which key fits this lock? (*Showing the keys*) Here are the keys I've been given and we are supposed to know which one opens this door and which one opens the inner door to the silver storeroom... Downstairs comes Lady Nerissa all hoity-toity. (*Turns to audience*) I call her "Bossy-big-boots" but not to her face...and she says, "Now you two, get those two caskets out of storage. The lead one and the silver one and bring them upstairs to the top chamber." (*Continues to speak to audience*) Now, we know there's an expensive jewelled casket too...our Lord, Portia's father, ordered it from Venice...it's gold and covered in precious jewels. (*Looks surreptitiously around*) It is kept in the secret closet in my Lady Portia's chamber with all her jewels...no burglar could ever find it. (*Lowers voice*) You see, as you go into her chamber, you turn left and just behind... (*Stops alarmed*) Oh no! I can't tell you...just in case there's a burglar listening, you never know these days...it's a wicked world out there...wicked. (*Turns to the other servant*) Let's see, I think this key opens the first door. (*Mimes the actions*) Good! Got it right. (*They go in and look around*) Honestly, there is so much stuff packed into this storeroom...look at this. (*Picking up an imagined helmet*) So old-fashioned no one is ever going to want to wear it. (*Puts it *down*) Right! Stay focused…lead casket. (*Looks around*) Ah, there it is. (*Mimes picking it up*) It weighs a ton…come on Giovanni… take it from me…don't just stand there! (*Mimes handing it over*) Yes! I know lead weighs a ton… I know it isn't fair…but life isn't fair… stop grumbling and take it up. Right, where is the key to the silver storeroom? (*Searches through the keys*) It's the key with the peculiar mark on it. (*Finds it*) Yes! (*As the servant moves forward, he/she steps on an old dress*) What is this? (*Bends down and picks it up*) A moth-eaten old dress. It should be thrown away even if it is made of velvet. (*Opens the door to the storeroom and goes in*) There's enough silver in here to sink a galleon. (*Looks around*) Ah! There it is… (*Taking a casket down from the shelf*) Needs a good clean, but it will shine up beautifully. (*Takes it outside and locks the door*) It doesn't weigh half as much as that ugly old lead one… (*Turning directly to audience*) Bet you anything it will be MY job to clean it!

At Lord Bassanio's Palazzo

The scene is set in the entrance hall of Lord Bassanio's palazzo in Venice, where Giovanni, one of his manservants, is stacking boxes and giving the audience an up-to-date account of the situation in the household.

GIOVANNI: (*Struggling with several boxes*) Go there...go here...what a state we've all been in since our Lord Bassanio got the money together to woo the Lady Portia...we thought he would never be able to cut a fine enough figure to go off to Belmont...such a magnificent palazzo overlooking the lagoon and much better than this dump, but his best friend, the Lord Antonio, came up trumps... it was all touch and go, so to speak...would he have sufficient money...well, not ready cash...not with his ships still at sea and waiting for their safe arrival from the Levant... He deals in spices and silks and is rich enough when ships dock safe and sound...but at present they are all at sea...and so, what does the Lord Antonio do? He goes off to the Rialto and borrows money off Shylock the Jew to give to my master the Lord Bassanio – his best friend – and now the whole household is in uproar with the preparations for the wooing...my Lord must have new gloves of the finest Moroccan leather, perfumed and lined with yellow silk and trimmed with gold lace...and to cut a fine figure – for he has mighty fine legs. He's ordered new boots too...in red Moroccan to match the gloves...and red is a most expensive colour. The deeper it is, the more it costs... and I was sent to tell the glover and the bootmaker to make them up of the deepest red money can buy...and here they are...all boxed up...ready to be matched with his doublet and hose...the tailor is with him now...giving him the last fitting...and what a marvellous sight...red and gold velvet with a fabulous cloak of red, lined with gold taffeta...the doge himself couldn't look finer. I'm telling you, my Lord Bassanio will be a most handsome and well-attired suitor… he's to travel up to Belmont in a gilded gondola…and arrive like a prince…he will put to shame all those others who come to woo that rich lady. And now I have to buy trinkets for all the servants, for my Lord Bassanio wishes to be generous…not content with coins, he wishes to give presents to them all at Belmont, and so I must rush here and there, buying up geegaws and such to distribute once we get there. And I am to have a new suit too…which you must agree I need…look at this (*he points to his hose*)…a hole! Made last week and not mended…but my Lord says I must be well dressed…not looking rundown and sad, so there's new hose and a new doublet for me (*He laughs*)…but not of red velvet an' silk…no, it's something more inferior and in green but, then, I am not a gentleman, but a gentleman's gentleman…and must accept my place in life… Oh! There's the evening curfew bell… I'd best get a move on with all these packages…the days ahead are going to be most interesting and exciting. (*He gathers them up*) Oh, yes, I'm taking bets on whether or not Lord Bassanio will be successful… (*He winks to the audience and starts to whistle as he exits*) I'm sure that I will win! When my Lady Portia set eyes on him a couple of months ago…wow, was she smitten. (*Winks again*) See you!

The Nurse's Boy, Verona

Peter is a houseboy in the Capulet palazzo in Verona. He has many jobs in the household. Juliet's nurse takes him with her on errands for her mistress. He has returned from a visit to Friar Lawrence's cell and is resting in the hall.

PETER: (*Wiping his forehead with his handkerchief*) I have been truly hot and bothered! We have been traipsing all over Verona, the nurse and I...in this heat...this part of Toscania has not known such heat these ten years or more...not since I was a nipper in my father's vineyard...yes! Before I was sent as kitchen boy to my Lord and Lady Capulet. What a different life from picking grapes – and slyly eating them – to running around for Cook in that great palazzo kitchen. The worse thing was turning the spit on a hot day and not being able to get away from the heat of those blazing logs. Oh, how I longed for a cool stream to paddle in, or the shade of my father's vines on the slope of a hill... Anyway, those days are now a long way off, and today I serve the household in a general way. Another job I hate is cleaning the women's *chopines* of mud, and mud is a polite word for all the stuff what gets stuck to them as they walk along. Come this noon time, our Lady Juliet's old nurse comes to me in the hall and says, "Come on Peter, it's you has to accompany me on an errand, so get off your fat..." (*He turns and points to his backside, tapping it*)...now, let's face it, that ain't fat, is it? And if you consider it is...well, I've seen fatter on a market day... like barrels (*He mimes a wide backside*)...and not just one or two, I can tell you! So, off we go, the nurse and I, to Friar Lawrence's cell, and is he there? No! So, we just hang around...and hang around... and it's hours before he shows up...gone off looking for some plant called feverfew, which deadens pain...well, by looking at his garden I would have thought he had every herb on God's earth growing there…and a big pile of manure. (*Waves hand under his nose and pulls a face of disgust*) Phew! Steaming away it was…rotting down ready to enrich the soil… I thought herbs grew in poor soil, well, that's what my pa used to say: "Poor soil, great herbs." But the friar might be growing something special in that garden of his that ain't just an 'erb…there's people say he's a miracle worker with his special potions and he makes lots of money for the abbey…and he knows secret recipes. Now, my Lady Juliet's nurse is an impatient sort of baggage and after we've been hanging around for some time, she says to me: "Right! Peter, we must go to the ropemaker on the Via Fortuna and order a rope ladder, so let's get going…it must be made up before curfew tonight and you can come an' get it for me…" An' I think, what does an arthriticky ol' woman like our nurse want with a rope ladder? She can hardly step up on a stool in our kitchen to get a jar of lemon balm ointment without huffing and puffing and saying her ol' joints are aching…so a rope ladder is a complete mystery to me…but then…this Capulet palazzo is a place full of mysteries…an' I trudge behind her hoping it's a short rope ladder she is ordering and not a long one…'cos I've got to go an' get it… (*He hears a bell toll*) That's the first curfew bell… I've got to get to the Via Fortuna before the second one sounds and bring back that blasted rope ladder…and, guess what? Nursey said, "Now, Peter, bring it in secret like and hide it in the kindling chest…and I will deal with it when I am ready…" What a mystery. (*He winks*) This place is full of mysteries…

Juliet's Nurse

The nurse's chamber in the Capulet palazzo in Verona. Nurse is in a tearful mood of regret as she folds clothes into a basket and shares her state of mind with the audience.

NURSE: My Lady Juliet was a lovely baby, sweet-tempered, not fractious like some – always crying and making a fuss. Even when she was teething, she just sucked on the big wooden teething beads I wore… sometimes I coated them in honey for her and she was even more content. It was my luck that my Lady Capulet kept me on…there are some families that just get rid of the wet nurse after the child has been weaned, but not the Capulets…no… I wasn't sent back to my village with a pension…no… I could stay with my lovely girl and bring her up. Lady Capulet always kept her distance…she's not the motherly type…and all she wants now is a fine marriage to a noble man…with my Juliet's enormous dowry, as she's their only child… she'll make the richest bride in Verona…that's why they gave that masked ball, to show off their wealth and lovely daughter…but why mask her face? That has confused me…but they wanted to show that Count Paris what wealthy friends they have…he arrived two days ago…and Lady Capulet wants my Juliet to be a countess so badly she's not going to allow Juliet any other options…when Juliet's mother sets her mind to it, there's no budging her…strong-minded is an understatement for her… Oh, but there's secrets in this palace only Juliet and I know of…and it makes me fearful… Romeo Montagu is at the heart of it! That masked ball was a bad idea, for it gave Romeo access to our forbidden world…a world free of Montagus…he should never have got in to woo my Lady Juliet (*wrings her hands in anguish*) and I have been wicked and connived at their union… Oh! At times, I wish I had been sent back to my village with a pension…not sent to Friar Lawrence's cell to arrange a marriage…a marriage! Married! Oh! What have I done? I ordered the rope ladder so Romeo could climb up to my Juliet's chamber. (*She wipes her eyes*) How could I do that knowing what might happen…but I have always been putty in her hands. My Lady Juliet is now a Montagu in a Capulet palace…her mother will go mad with rage…she would rather her daughter dead than titled a Montagu. And what of Count Paris? Lady Capulet will have Juliet married to him whether she likes it or not. But a secret can be kept a secret… I told my Lady Juliet she's had her night of wonderment with Romeo…a night that can last in her mind a lifetime…but now duty calls…obedience calls…the Bible commands we honour mother and father and Juliet must see reason… I have told her straight: pull yourself together, dry your tears, do your parents' bidding and marry the Count Paris…our secret can be kept. She listened to me, but there's a stubborn streak in Juliet… God knows what will happen next… (*Looking straight at the audience*) You had better say a prayer for the both of us…we need it!

(*She picks up her basket and leaves her chamber*)

In a Tiring Room at The Globe, 1599

A young boy actor sits in a dressing room backstage. He is preparing to play Juliet. At first, he sits at a table looking into an imagined mirror. With him is a tire-man (the name given to a man who helped the actors dress), who is helping him to get ready for a performance.

SAM: (*Rubbing an imagined cream into his face*) Whiter than white…white as a swan… Juliet must be like a swan with no blemish. (*Turning to his tire-man*) Yes! Tom, it's a good thing I never had the smallpox. It ruined the skin of our queen…mind, as old as she is now, does it matter? Old and wrinkled…old and decrepit…very well, Tom… I will be quiet…but you will not denounce me to the constable, will you? Good Thomas…we of the chamberlain's men must stick together, must we not? I must not forget my neck… Tom, show me Juliet's gown. I have forgot the neckline. (*He glances over at the imagined gown the tire-man holds up*) Ah! A square neckline…detail, Tom, it is all in the detail…we cannot have all those lords in the gallery sitting on their sixpenny stools saying I have "forgotten my chest"…or perhaps I should call it my "bosom"? (*He rubs the cream over the base of his neck*) There will be 700 stinkards* crammed into the open yard looking up at me, so I had better see that under my chin is also covered, Tom. Every detail matters…every little detail… there! Now for my wig, Tom. (*Taking the wig*) Ah! You have braided it well…that is exactly the braiding I like…gold to show Juliet's wealth…she is an heiress and lives in a palace. (*He fits the wig onto his head*) This wig is so much better than the one I had for Portia… I like this colour with the gold braid entwined…how could Romeo resist me with hair like this. (*He laughs and stands up*) Now for my gown. (*He mimes stepping into the gown and Tom fastens it from behind*) Red velvet. Oh! How I like red velvet. (*He turns around* *a few times*) Red velvet for the Capulet ball. No wonder Romeo won't take his eyes off me. Velvet trimmed with gold to match the braiding in my hair…now my shoes, Tom. (*He sits back at the table, mimes raising his gown and putting forward his feet*) These red-heeled shoes make me walk like a lady… (*He stands*) See, Tom, how I can now walk like the Lady Juliet Capulet of Verona. (*He shows off to Tom*) I am ready for those lords sitting on their sixpenny stools and penny extra cushions. (*He steps to the centre of the stage*)

> O Romeo, Romeo! Wherefore art thou Romeo?
> Deny thy father and refuse thy name;

And pray, Tom, that the bears do not howl and the dogs bark at the very moment of my speech and spoil the whole effect… I wish the city fathers would close down that flea-bitten, stinking bear garden over the wall…but that won't ever happen as it makes them too much money…vested interest, Tom, the world is all about money. Now, I am ready to face my audience…

*A slang word used to describe the groundlings who paid a penny to stand and watch the play; the smell created "a big stink".

Cholera, 1838

Jack is a young blacksmith's apprentice. He sits, dejectedly, on a bench outside the forge, eating bread and cheese and drinking from a small mug, as he tells the audience about the tragedy that hit his family.

JACK: Me ma and pa died of that cholera what come to town last year...
a terrible sickness it was. Hundreds of people died in the lower
town. Those what live up on the hill, the rich, that is, did not suffer
half as much as we poor souls in the Sandfields. They say it's the
smells from the poor that makes it grow. My boss, what 'as a bit of
learning, says the mayor announced that it was a miasma that grows
out of the filth and stench in our part of town... I like the sound
of miasma, but it was a killer... I was lucky, 'cos my ma was 'avin'
another baby and sent me up the valley to live with me gran 'cos there
was no more room in the 'ouse me pa rented. Ma thought I could
live with Gran for a bit...there was seven of us in two bedrooms,
if two bedrooms you can call 'em. Mind you, we was lucky to 'ave
stairs...some on our road just had ladders to the room above...you
can fall off ladders, easy like. Gran kept me busy all summer an' we
'ave no news of the dreadful horrors of the town. I enjoys meself up
in the valley... I like goats see, an' Gran puts me in charge of all 'er
goats. Goat's milk I have to drink, an' goat's cheese for me dinner.
Gran even calls me 'er billy goat, jokey like, an' says I'll grow into
one if I'm to think so much on them. All night I sleeps in a bed
all to meself, no girls' elbows to stick in me sides or wriggling toes
to scratch me legs. A bed all to meself I 'as at Gran's, a box-bed
in the kitchen, all nice an' warm...spoiled I am on a cold night.
Then come September end, after the gleaning time, I goes home,
seven miles down the valley I comes, an' I finds they're all dead.
All of them. I can 'ardly believe my eyes an' ears...our old house

is all locked up, empty, the furniture gone to pay for coffins. Our neighbours, those that 'ave survived the sickness, tells me me family all died in the cholera time. I stares at them in amazement...me ma an' pa dead...an' the four little 'uns what I left behind... I couldn't speak, I was so taken aback with the grief of it...they not be wicked folks, not like some of those in the Sandfields what drinks, an' fights an' swears... But God took 'em...and I only wishes now that they be all safe in 'eaven where no wickedness may reach 'em and that the angelic choir sings to 'em all day. So, with my grief, back I trailed up the valley to Gran... Gran an' me cried bitter tears many a night when we thought about our losses. That was an 'ard winter...we used up all our logs pretty fast...at the end of it Gran says she 'as saved ten shillings, coin of the realm, an' all in silver pieces from selling her goat's cheese in the market near us...an' that will go to me being bound apprentice to our blacksmith at 'is forge...an' that's what I do now, worthy work it is, but when the flames flare up, and he strikes the anvil 'ard, it's faces I see in the flames, the faces of the little 'uns...with the cholera, and I shed many a tear.

Sticking, 1860

The scene is set in a country lane alongside an estate wall. Bobbit has been collecting wood for the fire back at the family cottage. It is not easy to find sticks, as the whole village needs firewood on a daily basis just to boil a kettle.

BOBBIT: Oh! That was a near miss. (*Breathless, from running down the lane*) I thought 'e'd got me that time. (*Puts bundle of sticks down and rests*) But thank God, I'm faster and can run like a whippet when I need to! Squire's gamekeeper should keep 'is mind on pheasants and coneys, not worry about us villagers sticking. What's a bundle of sticks to our squire anyway? My pa says 'e's got 500 acres from the rail station to Throxton Gibbet an' Squire's more like a king in these parts. We've only 'ad our railway 'bout two years. The squire made such a fuss, 'e didn't want no railway and no station neither...not that great big, smoky, belching machine rushing through 'is estate and frightening the game...frightening 'er Ladyship more likely 'cos she do suffer from those megrims what gentlewomen do 'ave most of the time. Squire refused to 'ave the railway but the government made 'im give up the land, an' 'e got thousands of pounds compensation... think on that, thousands of pounds... Why, the whole village could be kept in firewood forever with what Squire got! No one need go sticking... I breaks me back sometimes bending down looking for bits and pieces... Mind, when the wind blows, as it does mightily in these parts, we gets trees blown down in Squire's plantation, an' it's a scramble to get in first and grab the wood. There was a great storm last February...that time of year is awful round these parts. Through the night there was a-blowin' and a-blusterin' an' the whole village could hear Squire's trees a-creakin' an' fallin'. The next day, our gran is up at the crack of dawn, sharp like, to do stickin'...she gets down to the wood in no time an' finds a lot of ol' branches what's come down…well, our gran is a champion sticker…she can pick up sticks faster than five gran'children all put together and makes up bundles fast and ties them with binder string… Gran is so 'ard concentratin' on 'er stickin' that she don't hear 'er Ladyship in 'er grand manner sayin', "Gran Thatcher, you stop thieving Squire's wood! You'll be up before the magistrate if you're not careful. You know this is our home park and villagers are not allowed to go sticking here!" Gran was that upset, mortified, she threw down the bundle of sticks she 'ad and said she was very sorry. Who'd 'ave thought Her Ladyship would be trampin' through the woods at that time with 'er Berlin pugs…four of them she 'ad and nasty blowed up eyes they got, bulging out. Well, she gave Gran a piece of 'er mind and made Gran promise she'd never go into the wood again (fat chance of that, I can tell you) and Gran had to climb back over the wall with 'er Ladyship an' those pugs watchin' 'er. Mind you, Gran 'ad the last laugh, 'cos she'd thrown three bundles of sticks already over the wall, an' 'er Ladyship didn't know that! Gran came 'ome 'appy as a lark with all those bundles of sticks…she couldn't care tuppence about 'er Ladyship nor 'er pugs…and we all 'ad blazing fires for our tea…and this lot… (*picking up the bundle of sticks*) is to 'eat up Ma's saucepan…give it a good boil…for our supper tonight…

The Ghetto Kid, 1945

This scene is based on historical records. It is set in a Polish orphanage near the end of World War II. Danya is a Jewish girl who has been sheltered by nuns from the Nazi occupiers. One night, she managed to escape the Jewish ghetto in Warsaw through the sewers; her parents were left behind to perish. Here, she speaks directly to the audience about her escape and survival.

DANYA: My real name is Danya. It's a Hebrew name meaning 'judgement of God'. But it is too Jewish, so the Polish lady who pulled me from the sewer told me to forget it…forget everything, she said…forget you are a Jewish girl…from now on, you are Anna Karwacinski… that was my new name. (*She starts to cry*) In the ghetto, my mother had taken me to a sewer that connected with the outside…when she lifted the iron grille the smell was revolting. I said, "No! Mama. No! Mama. Don't tell me to go into that hole…it is a stinking hole…" And not only that, it was a black hole…like a stinking mouth. But she held me tight and said, "It is your only chance, Danya. You will die if you stay in the ghetto. I want you to live and to remember us…remember…memory is life…you will give us life beyond this…" She was sobbing and I was sobbing…then she whispered, "Listen, go down and when you reach the bottom, turn to the left. Remember to go left, you must go left." I was only six, but I knew my left from my right because I had been taught to put my own shoes on… "When you see a shaft of light coming down… and it will seem a long way…go to the iron ladder and a lady will be waiting for you." And that's how it was…but I was soaking… soaking in horrible muck…unmentionable muck, you know… I was filthy… The lady took me to a safe place. It was dark and there was a German curfew in the city…but we made it. When we got to her apartment, she wanted to clean me up…she had to do that before passing me on. But there was no soap...soap had become a precious thing by then...so, she went to a neighbour and got some...that was dangerous...if she aroused suspicion the Gestapo could have come. When I was cleaned up and given new clothes, I was told I would become a Christian girl... Forget everything! Forget the Torah...my memories had to be kept in here. (*She taps her head*) Never voiced... never spoken...the lady gave me some papers...my new identity... and then took me to the nuns who ran the orphanage... I am a Christian girl named Anna Karwacinski... I have to learn very fast in case there is an inspection...the catechism...the Lord's Prayer... I have to attend Mass...forget the Torah. This orphanage is full of secrets...we do not share them...my new life started when I learned the Lord's Prayer...that lady's name I never knew...names are dangerous...the less we know the better...it is an orphanage where secrets are kept even by the nuns...and no one asks questions... silence means safety...and I repeat with absolute conviction, "Our Father, who art in heaven, hallowed be thy name..." But now they say the Germans have gone and the Russians are coming...will I be able to be Danya again? I am very scared...the nuns are scared too, as the Russians are Bolsheviks... Communists who hate the Church. Who knows what will happen to us now...we all say our prayers.

Recruiting, 1914

This scene is set in a field in Kent. A young woman in a riding habit carries a crop and a small bag. She stands to one side of the acting area, where a young agricultural worker mimes digging and hoeing, at first paying no attention to her.

LUCY: I feel it is my patriotic duty to ride around our estate and get the young farm hands to join up. (*To one side of the acting area, a young man is digging and hoeing*) What use is it, if our men miss their chance? The estate can function quite well with the older men doing their jobs. Indeed, some of the old codgers who live on Papa's generosity can jolly well pull their socks up and pitch in to do some farm work…the old men can take over from the young men. (*She sees the young labourer as he mimes his task*) You are Ted Harris, are you not? From Home Farm?

TED: (*Stopping his work and doffing his cap*) Yes, Miss Lucy, we be Sir Andrew's tenants… I have to clear this half acre of weeds by nightfall… I've been at it since daybreak. (*He motions to the field*) I've been most diligent, as they be a great number of nettles.

LUCY: (*Ignoring the field*) You know that we are at war with Germany since August 4th…the Huns are murdering Belgian mothers and children every day…indeed, every hour…

TED: Yes! I read my pa's newspaper every night after he's finished with it…

LUCY: Then you know all about the atrocities that are being committed right across poor defenceless Belgium.

TED: Ay! They be mounting up all week… Pa gets angry about Belgian babies stuck on German bayonets…

LUCY: Then why are you not in uniform? I have been marching around Canterbury handing out white feathers to those young men still in civilian clothes… I hadn't realised there were so many cowards in the town…and I still have a whole bag of white feathers here. (*She holds up a bag*) But, I am sure you will do your duty, Ted…yes…do the right thing and join up before it's too late and all over…

TED: We heard that Sir Andrew's two footmen have gone to the recruiting centre in town.

LUCY: Yes, they have! We couldn't have them lazing around the manor when there's a war on. We intend only to have female staff for the near future.

TED: My sister Meg will be pleased to hear that…she'll be thirteen next month and hopes to join Cook in the manor kitchen. (*Starts miming digging*) This field isn't going to be free of weeds with me jawing about my sister…

LUCY: (*Irritated*) But Ted, what are you going to do about the war?

TED: (*He stops working*) Well, Miss Lucy, it's like this; my pa says I should go but my ma is dead against it. When I bring up the subject, she starts to cry because her brother got killed in the Boer War…and she says it's the politicians' fight, not ours, and she starts to cry bitterly.

LUCY: The Boer War was a silly little African war! This is much bigger, and it's across the Channel, not in Africa…

TED: Anyway, Miss Lucy, I only be sixteen.

LUCY: That's old enough. Indeed, you look much older. You could be mistaken for eighteen at least… I am sure once you are in uniform, your ma will be proud of you.

TED: My ma says I'm too short for the army anyways…

LUCY: Nonsense! Five foot six is tall enough to serve…and you must be five foot seven at least. So, that's big enough…off you go…be brave, Ted.

(*Ted picks up his spade and hoe and marches off*)

LUCY: (*Calling after Ted*) That's the right thing to do…fight the Huns for us all…it's a job well done…get in before it's all over, Ted…be brave!

Rats

Two men crouch in a World War I front line trench. There is a lull in the action and the men are having a smoke. (If possible, the sound of shelling should be heard in the background throughout the scene)

TED: (*Having a drag on his cigarette*) You know what? I never imagined it would be like this…

ARTHUR: Like what?

TED: Stuck in a muddy hole for weeks on end.

ARTHUR: This ain't a hole, it's a trench.

TED: Call it what you will, mate, it's just a deep muddy hole that zigzags along and we're stuck in part of it.

ARTHUR: Yeah! And it's going to be Christmas and this war ain't over.

TED: (*Taking another long drag on his cigarette*) And it looks like going on forever…

ARTHUR: I bet the generals get their Christmas dinner all laid on posh like.

TED: Any minute now, Captain Wentworth will show up blowing his shrill whistle and telling us to get up and go…

ARTHUR: Are you ready to go?

TED: I'll go when I've had my rum ration.

ARTHUR: I reckon we are safe…there's no sign of the rum jars…let's crouch down deeper, mate.

TED: This trench is one hell of a muddy maze. (*He crouches deeper*) And it's full of bloody rats.

ARTHUR: (*Looking around*) Yeah, tell me about it. I bet there's ten rats to every man.

TED: Probably more…and as big as cats… I hate them…they get big on eating dead horses…

ARTHUR: Say the truth…it's not only dead horses they feed on…

TED: Yeah…dead men too…but I'm not going to tell my ma that.

ARTHUR: It gives me the horrors thinking of the rats gnawing at our dead mates out there in no man's land…

TED: Yeah…rat heaven.

ARTHUR: (*Laughing about it*) Mind you…the German shells can blow them to smithereens too… God! We get a shower of dead rats as we move forward.

TED: No wonder they give us rum!

ARTHUR: Dutch courage, mate.

TED: Yeah…human life and a rat's life are cheap out here…

ARTHUR: Don't forget the poor horses, they get killed too…mutilated by the shells, just like us…

TED: I thought I saw my squire's hunter the other day…a sorry sight, covered in mud and shivering with fear.

ARTHUR: Poor buggers…carriage horses, thoroughbreds, hunters all requisitioned…they get frightened as we do when the Huns give us hell!

TED: Our squire's daughter, Miss Lucy, always rode a beautiful strawberry roan mare…she's probably been requisitioned and Miss Lucy can't go riding no more.

ARTHUR: (*Suddenly getting alarmed and pointing at a corner*) Good God! Look at the size of that rat…there…look! It's the size of a cat…

TED: You're jittery…rats are a fact of life…

ARTHUR: Not rats the size of a cat!

TED: At home we had a ratting terrier. She was a champion ratter.

ARTHUR: Stop nattering and get a spade…that's why the captain has his terrier with him…officer's privilege.

TED: (*Mimes getting a spade and starts hitting the rat*) This spade will smash him to a pulp. (He hits the imaginary rat) Get that, you bugger. You know where there's one of these there will be ten…

ARTHUR: I hated rats at home and hate them even more here…they don't even run away, they come for you!

(*Ted finishes killing the rat and puts the spade down*)

TED: (*Shivering and rubbing his hands together*) This cold is getting to me…

into my bones…freezing them… I could do with a nice cuppa tea.

ARTHUR: There's nothing nice about the tea we get here! They put too much chloride in the water to kill the germs…water like that ain't going to make nice tea!

TED: You're always complaining…can't you be cheerful for once?

ARTHUR: What's cheerful about this? There's a lot to complain about. If I had a choice, I'd have extra rum ration and put it in my tea. Rum would cheer me up no end, even if it's half a gill…

TED: If they put lots of sugar in it, you don't taste the lime so much. Tea warms you up…it's a nice comforter.

ARTHUR: Rum would warm you up quicker, mate.

TED: Let's face it…the Huns chuck everything they can at us and we'll have to just grin and bear it…

ARTHUR: And drink our bloody tea!

(*There is silence*)

TED: Hang on, Arthur…it's silent, there's no barrage…hey! Can you hear it? The Huns are singing…

(*From the German lines, the sound of 'Heilige Nacht' can be heard*)

ARTHUR: We can do better than that…let's show 'em, Ted.

(*The men sing 'Silent Night' together in reply to the Germans. If possible, the two versions blend together in unison*)

Nursing the Wounded

This scene is set in a military hospital near the Western Front in 1916. We see a Voluntary Aid Detachment (VAD) nurse sitting at a table with medical supplies.

LUCY: (*Carefully rolling up bandages and putting them into a basket*) The war has been going on for two years. We never expected it to drag on and on in this way...endlessly. (*Wiping away tears*) My parents were against my joining the VADs and coming over to France but I had to assuage my feelings of guilt. You can't imagine the depths of my self-hatred. (*She wipes away more tears*) To think that I was rash enough to hand out white feathers in Canterbury. That I rode around my father's estate and urged our young men to fight for 'king and country'! I made them feel like cowards... I called them cowards. (*Starts to cry again*) I had it in my stupid head that it would all be glorious, simply glorious, and over by Christmas! Oh! How my words and actions haunt me now. Do you hear the guns? It never, ever stops...pounding...thudding...on and on, and each time they bring in a new load of wounded the guilt returns to me. Young men, seventeen, eighteen years of age, with their young bodies shattered, mutilated, their frightened eyes meeting mine. The guilt surges up in me while I sit beside a bed, holding the hand of a young man who is dying, and I have to be composed...nurse-like, but he's frightened and wants his ma, and all I can do is squeeze his hand and pretend that he will pull through! But all I want to do is cry with him, for him and for myself...the guilt is always there...terrible guilt! Made worse by the fact that there are no more beds available, they are all taken, so we make the wounded as comfortable as we can on the floor...the floor! They bring in wounded German soldiers too and Matron asks me to deal with them because I speak German. It's a comfort to them, especially the really bad cases, with no hope. (*She wipes her eyes*) I always open the windows when they die to let their souls go out. Here we are, nursing the prisoners and getting just as upset when they die in horrible pain as we do when our chaps die... they don't seem to be the enemy when I'm holding the hand of a young Bavarian man who is dying of sepsis and wanting his mother so badly... An English hand, a German hand...they're all the same, they're mostly young, nineteen, twenty, my age...and they're dying and need comforting...loving one soldier and hating the other... the enemy...isn't in my nature. Ich kann sie nicht hassen, weil sie sterben.* (*She is overcome with emotion*) I will never, ever be able to forget all of this...

*I cannot hate them as they die.

A Soldier with a Plan, 1917

A soldier crouches down in a front line trench. In the background, there is the sound of an incessant barrage.

BEN: (*Crouching down and shaking his head*) Lies, all lies! The war wasn't over by Christmas…it has been ongoing hell for all of us. Each of us cowering in our own private misery, hoping there will be a day when the rum won't appear…with the rum comes the order to "get up and go"! And up the scaling ladders we have to go and march… or run…into hell… I like days when there's no rum! I get the shivers all right when Lieutenant Wentworth appears with the sergeant shouting, "Up and over, boys! Give the Bosch hell!" and we all go scrambling out of the trench into no man's land. They should call it 'dead man's land', that's the truth of it. The mates you had and didn't get back are all out there rotting away. And I don't mean neat dead bodies all intact. I mean bits of bodies…shells that blew their heads off… (*he gets emotional*)…split their skulls apart…sometimes we have to run over them, not only our boys, but Huns too…it's hell, the shells, the German machine guns mowing us all down… the Huns are throwing all they can at us…the ground shakes like jelly under your feet. (*Wipes away a tear*) I can't take this anymore. However many fags I smoke, my nerves are shattered. Some days, I can't stop shaking…but I've got a plan…in five days' time I'm due for leave to Blighty. I'll be home and my ma's gone as cook to Bromley Manor…she can hide me in one of the gardener's sheds on the estate. All the gardeners have enlisted…the gardens have gone to rack and ruin…overgrown…so, I'll hide meself, desert and not come back…they shoot you here for desertion, but at home in Blighty they just send you to prison. They have to find you first and no one knows where my ma has gone to work…sometimes it pays to be

Mrs Jones… Lord Bromley's gone and given the manor over to the army as a convalescent home for wounded soldiers, so no one's going to notice me arriving, and I can bandage meself up a bit and then I disappear. Ma says no one goes into the gardens…no one cares… it's a shambles… I could hide and be safe there until this bloody war is over… Our trench fills up with water, it is damn freezing and I don't want to get trench foot and have my legs amputated before I puts my plan into action…please God, don't let me be killed or get trench foot…save me so I can get back to Blighty…

The Rum Ration?

Two officers are seated at a table in their dugout, looking at a line-up of jars that have just arrived. Bombing can be heard in the distance.

WENTWORTH: (*Tapping one of the jars with his officer's stick*) This new delivery of jars doubles our rum ration for the men, sir!

CAPTAIN: We weren't ready for yet more rum, Wentworth. It's a mystery to me. We'll have to stack them up with the others.

WENTWORTH: Mysteries are rather worrying, are they not, sir?

CAPTAIN: These jars look brand new. (*Picking one up*) Not at all like refills…jars that get knocked about a bit.

WENTWORTH: The men love their rum ration, sir. There'd be trouble if we ran out of the stuff…better to have a top-up.

Captain: (*Un-corking a jar*) I've never fancied rum myself. (*He sniffs at the contents and grimaces*) Good God! This stuff smells disgusting. (*Shaking his head*) It's worse than the smell of gangrene and that's bad enough. (*He offers Wentworth the jar*) Take a sniff of that, Wentworth…

WENTWORTH: Rather not, sir, if you don't mind…take your word for it…absolutely…you're always right, sir!

CAPTAIN: What on earth are they expecting us to do with this ghastly stuff… (*Irritated*) And what on earth is it?

WENTWORTH: Can't say, sir. Shall we open the envelope that came with the jars?

CAPTAIN: Good idea… Throw some light on this delivery!

WENTWORTH: (*Opens the envelope and quickly scans its contents*) It seems, sir, that the jars are full of whale oil!

CAPTAIN: Whale oil? Fighting a war with rum rations I can understand but I thought whale oil was used to make soap!

WENTWORTH: (*Sifting through the papers*) It might be useful to see what our orders are... (*He finds the relevant page and reads it*) Wait 'til you read these orders, sir!

CAPTAIN: You read them to me, Wentworth. I don't know where my glasses are.

WENTWORTH: Right, sir!

CAPTAIN: I can't wait to hear what we have to do with this disgusting stuff not make soap for the troops, I hope!

WENTWORTH: You won't believe the orders, sir...

CAPTAIN: I will believe anything that comes from headquarters...

WENTWORTH: Then, what do you think of these orders, sir? (*He reads carefully*) "Because of the intense cold prevalent at this time, the following is advised for all men: before going out on patrol in these dire weather conditions, each man must be stripped of his clothes and rubbed with whale oil by an officer. This procedure will help to keep each man warm and prevent his body from freezing. An officer must see that it is done thoroughly."

CAPTAIN: (*Shocked*) God forbid, Wentworth! What will headquarters think of next?

WENTWORTH: God only knows, sir, but what man would stand there naked and have an officer rub him down like a horse?

CAPTAIN: The men would refuse...it's a damn insult!

WENTWORTH: The men would feel humiliated...

CAPTAIN: Yes! Greasing them up like a cooking pan...we would have a mutiny on our hands...

WENTWORTH: Well, you could include me, sir! As I am not rubbing whale oil on any of my men...

CAPTAIN: But we would be disobeying orders. (*Thinking about the problem*) Got it! We could say it never seemed cold enough for the men to freeze.

WENTWORTH: I think I have a better solution, sir. We have to get rid of this horrible stuff...so, why don't we tell our men that the whale oil is to prevent trench foot and amputations. The men fear losing their feet to gangrene so we could order them to rub the oil into their own feet and up their legs...that way, they do it themselves.

CAPTAIN: (*Overjoyed*) Cracking idea, Wentworth! Good man! The men can do all their own rubbing…it will give them something to do occupy their time… (*He laughs uproariously*) We can empty the jars in no time at all and get rid of the ghastly stuff.

WENTWORTH: Let's hope when we send these jars back empty to headquarters, they don't get used for the rum ration by mistake…

CAPTAIN: (Pouring himself a drink) That's why I'm sticking to Cognac. Will you join me, Wentworth? (He pours another drink and hands it over) Here's to 'problem-solving'. (He raises his glass) Two heads are better than one, eh?

WENTWORTH: Absolutely right, sir!

Whale Oil for the Troops

A group of soldiers is gathered in the reserve trench. There is bombardment at a distance, and the men are relaxing. They have their boots off and are applying whale oil to their feet.

LEN: When the sarge appeared with these jars, I thought we was getting a rum ration. When he said this stuff is to prevent trench foot I couldn't believe it…but I'd love a drop of rum while I'm doing this…give me rum any day…

EDWIN: Not in the reserve trench, mate!

LEN: This stuff smells God-awful… (*He applies the oil*)

EDWIN: I'd put anything on my feet to prevent trench foot.

LEN: How much do you think we have to put on?

EDWIN: How the hell would I know? The sarge said, "Plaster it on you lot and get on with it snappy quick, rub it in well between your toes…"

LEN: The trench foot amputees get sent home to Blighty.

EDWIN: So, you think they're lucky going home with no feet? On bloody crutches for the rest of their lives!

(*The men are silent as they work the whale oil into their feet and ankles*)

LEN: I hope this stuff washes off easily before we go on leave to Blighty.

EDWIN: Do you think Lieutenant Wentworth is putting whale oil on his feet?

LEN: Not on your nellie, mate! He's probably been issued with crème-de la-crème-de-bloody-lavender…

EDWIN: I like the sound of that stuff!

(*The men rub more oil on their feet and ankles*)

LEN: (*Laughing*) And the captain has eau-de-perfume de violets de Paris.

EDWIN: You seem to know a lot about nice smells…

LEN: (*Giving a knowing smile*) Well, I've been around a lot of nice smelling women…there's not a lot you can spend your money on, is there? Plonk and women back at Armentier.

EDWIN: (Smiling) Hey! You'd better not tell your ma.

LEN: There's a lot of things I don't tell my ma about. She's a Wesleyan
Methodist, but she's a long way from the fun in Armentier!
(*The men finish rubbing the oil and put their socks and boots back on as
the banter continues. In the background, the sound of an accordion can
be heard from the German trench*)

EDWIN: There he goes again, that Bavarian accordion player. He's good,
very good.

LEN: How close do you think he is?

EDWIN: Maybe sixty yards away.

LEN: And how do you know he's Bavarian? They're all Huns to me!

EDWIN: Last time we went over, the uniforms had changed. Germany is
made up of different states. A Bavarian isn't the same as a Prussian…
a Prussian is nastier.

LEN: How do you know so much? They didn't teach us all that at my
school. It was all Germany and the Kaiser and they're all Huns.

EDWIN: I was footman to Lord Litchfield. You pick up a lot when you're
waiting at table. Our so-called 'betters' are big talkers, especially the
men when the ladies go off to have their coffee and the men get their
port going round the table.

LEN: So, that's why you got nice hands then! 'Cos you handed the upper
classes their port…posh bastards! And they're going to be even nicer
with whale oil! (*Laughs*)

EDWIN: These? (*He holds up his hands*) They're not so nice now. (*He
laughs*) Lord Litchfield wouldn't have me waiting at table with hands
like these! But we all wore white gloves in the dining room, so he
wouldn't see the dirt under my fingernails, would he? (*He laughs
ironically*) This is a different world…and he sent us all out of the
dining room when it was time for the port. They could speak freely
then and they got right noisy telling their tales…passed the port
round themselves…they didn't want us hearing what they said.

LEN: I would think there's differences in each household. Talking of
toffs…look who's coming down our trench…

EDWIN: Lieutenant Wentworth, he's not too bad. He's probably coming to check that we've used that whale oil on our feet. He doesn't talk down to us like we're scum…

LEN: A toff's a toff. I bet he's got his nice expensive body armour on. Money buys safety; our khaki is a death dress.

EDWIN: Oh, cheer up! Lieutenant Wentworth doesn't speak to us like a bunch of schoolboys…

LEN: And anyway, he's gone down the side trench…

EDWIN: Come on, let's have a singsong. Get your mouth organ out, Len.

LEN: Here we go… (*He starts to play 'What a friend we have in Jesus'*)

EDWIN: (*Picks up the tune but sings different words*)

"When this lousy war is over,
Oh, how happy we will be,
When I get my civvy clothes on,
No more soldiering for me,
No more church parades on Sunday,
No more putting in for leave,
I will kiss the sergeant major,
How I'll miss him, how I'll grieve."

LEN: (*Stops playing*) I enjoyed that. We're good mates…and, Edwin, you have a good voice.

Mustard Gas, 1917

A soldier stands alone in a trench. The pounding of guns can be heard in the background.

SOLDIER: This war rages on, it is unceasing…we fight our battles, gain a few yards…a village if we're lucky, but it's stalemate, I tell you… the German spirit seems undimmed and there is no weakening of their defences…however much we throw at them, it still ends up stalemate…but after three years of fighting on two fronts they need a decisive victory and that's why we are now enduring a new weapon…a new terrible weapon that the Huns have manufactured. It's lethal…it terrifies us. When the first mustard gas came over, we were utterly unprepared. It's odourless and takes it's time creeping along…lethal…getting into every corner of a trench and we cannot get away from it…to say it terrified us is an understatement. It is inhuman, barbarous, even worse than being machine gunned down or burned to a cinder by one of their flamethrowers who appear like demons out of hell! The Scots further up our trench have been in a bad way…we call them kilties. They're proud of their kilts, but it's terrible for them in a gas attack; the mustard gas burns their legs and their bare bums something terrible. Imagine the horror of it all, the scorching, burning sensations and nothing can be done to stop it once it hits…but now we've been issued with these. (*Holds up a gas mask*) Some of us have been lucky, but it's too late for some of the kilties further down the trench who are now blinded…burned and totally blind. This morning I was on stand-to. There I was with my gas mask on, listening to myself breathing. It is a strange sensation…your head is encased and you try to breathe and peer out through the eye glasses… I want to take it off, I want to be able to breathe unhindered. When we all have our gas masks on, we inhabit

a strange world of fellow zombies, but it's better to be a zombie than totally unprotected. It was awful to see the horses blinded by the mustard gas, totally unprotected as we were…but now they have gas masks too, but they play up and snort when they see them coming… they hate them as much as we do. (*He puts his mask on*)
(*A disembodied upper-class voice can be heard issuing instructions*)
"If you are unfortunately caught in a gas attack without a gas helmet, the army issues these instructions which all men will strictly follow:

1. Take out your handkerchief
2. Urinate into the material until it is soaked completely and utterly
3. Tie it around your mouth and nose very tightly and breathe through it.

This procedure, if followed correctly, will help you get through the mustard attack."
(*He pulls off his mask*)
What stupid instructions we get…the gas is odourless, we can't smell it and it takes time to get out a handkerchief, that's if you've got one, undo your flies, pee in your hankie and then tie it around your nose and mouth! The generals must be fucking joking or completely mad…and I reckon they're both…yeah! Fucking mad!

Horses and Men

A young officer sits at a table with letters on it. There is the sound of a bombardment in the distance.

WENTWORTH: Through the horror of our daily situations, I try not to think of how it is, but we are all war-weary, exhausted…three years of death and casualties, one's brothers, cousins dead…so many old school chums killed, with no end in sight. All this carnage. At times, it seems that God has forsaken us; but we are forbidden to think that! No! We must not think that and just carry on, but… It's the shooting of the horses that tears at my heartstrings. I have always loved horses and this is a war of horses and men…we could not function without the horses, but sometimes they slide, lose their footing and sink into the mud-filled craters…it's a slippery hell and we cannot get them out. I see the fear in their eyes as they snort and struggle, but there's nothing we can do. Only an officer can shoot them, so my men come for me and I have to get out my revolver and shoot the terrified animal…and it's all… (*he struggles with his emotions*)…it's all so bloody awful, and I want to cry, but I can't in front of the men. It has to be 'businesslike'…the regulation revolver shot and another horse dead, and I cannot even compose myself by breathing in fresh air. (*He shakes his head despondently*) There's no such thing as fresh air, it's all polluted with smoke, gun smoke, barrage smoke, cordite, the stink from the latrines, rat urine, our urine…there is no such thing as clean fresh air. I sometimes think that I shall never ever breathe in anything sweet ever again. Oh! How I long for clear, sweet, pure fresh air… (*He struggles with his emotions*) The Huns chuck everything they can at us and we just have to grin and bear it, and breathe in the stench, and I try not to look at the mutilated bodies of the horses everywhere.

I must try not to dwell on this…

The mail has come in. It was brought up on the ammunition limbers. I heard the cry "Mail up" and then the running feet of the men. The mail is brought up at night but the men have to unload the ammunition before they get their mail. You should see them working at speed along a chain as they pass the shells swiftly to the gun pits. We officers have to sit still and wait for our letters to be brought to us by our servants. It's a sore trial to our patience, part of the price we pay for our rank…we are all desperate for news, something to take our minds off the present situation… (*He picks up a letter*) It's odd to think how far these letters travel and how safely they arrive, despite being brought up under shellfire. The men line up to get them…letters from their mothers, their wives, their sweethearts. Once they're distributed, the men sit around their fires in silence, reading by the light of the jumping flame…the war seems to have ceased for a little while, while the men's memories are back in Blighty, affections stirring…it's the only link they have with the life they've left behind. (*He looks through some of the letters on the table*) Such precious things, these letters. I watch the captain's face sometimes as he reads his. Sometimes it seems they do not tell him what he wants to hear. (*He shrugs*) But I don't question him, and he never tells me what he has read…well… (*He slices open one of his letters*) I think I'll read my mother's first…thank God, she has no idea what life is really like here…she thinks I'm a hero doing my duty… (*He struggles to stop himself crying*) She has no idea how hellish it is…if she did, she would cry for me… (*He looks at his mother's letter*) And she would write me a different sort of letter…

Going Home to Blighty, 1918

The scene is a World War I trench. It is 1918 and the war on the Western Front seems to be never-ending. British and German troops face each other across a stretch of land called no man's land. Two young soldiers stand in a corner of the trench, detached from the others in their regiment.

TAFFY: (*Stamping and shifting his feet around*) If I don't stamp around, this mud seems to really suck me down. Turns to muddy cement, it does. Really nasty stuff.

RON: It's not half as deep as that trench outside of Messines. The mud was up to my armpits…

TAFFY: That's an exaggeration, isn't it?

RON: OK, up to my waist! Will that satisfy your 'delicate sense of gaining factual information'?

TAFFY: There's no need to get shirty with me, Ron. A fact is a fact.

RON: Well, as I was stuck in a trench for over a week with nothing happening, it felt like the mud was rising up and overwhelming me, smothering me even…

TAFFY: You'll be telling me next that the rats were bigger than cats. (*He gestures with his arms*) "As big as this, Taffy! The biggest rats you've ever seen!"

RON: (*Angrily*) Well, they were, I can tell you! Well fed on our boys' corpses… I hate rats…they get big on dead horses too.

TAFFY: Don't let's talk about it. It gives me the shivers…
(*Silence*)

RON: Hey! Have you still got your old Princess Royal tin? (*He gets a small tin out of his pocket*) Mine's full of fags…

TAFFY: Yeah! Isn't it nice to know the Princess Mary was thinking about us?

RON: (*Miming Taffy*) "Isn't it nice to know the Princess Mary was thinking about us!" Look, mate, the princess couldn't have cared less. It's all political manipulation, isn't it? Keep the troops happy, con them into thinking the royal family is thinking about them stuck in the trenches. "We, the royals, are with each and every one of you brave boys. We shall send you a little tin of goodies to keep you happy."

TAFFY: I liked what I got in my tin. Now I keep my fags in it too.

RON: Cannon fodder! That's what we are. Come the revolution and they'll all be swept away. Gone! And good riddance to them!

TAFFY: That's a bit harsh, Ron.

RON: Look boyo, the British royals are all Germans, and here we are still facing Germans. Behind that barbed wire are all their German cousins, trying to kill us...bloody Bosch!

(*Silence*)

TAFFY: Wilf down the line had a lucky escape. He showed me his pocket Bible what he keeps in his breast pocket. We were queued up for the latrines...

RON: (*Contemptuously*) Ugh! A Bible carrier...

TAFFY: It has a big hole in the middle. It stopped a bullet. Wilf says it was God directing his guardian angel to keep him safe. It touched his skin but stopped in his Bible.

RON: (*Laughing*) It wasn't God. It wasn't his guardian angel. It was just bloody luck! Get it Taffy, good luck!

TAFFY: Don't you believe in God, Ron?

RON: I'm an atheist. I'm not here because of king and country, or God. I'm here because I got bloody conscripted. Got it?

(*Silence*)

TAFFY: Well, I pray all the time that God will keep me safe. My ma would die of a broken heart if I didn't get back.

RON: Boyo, I'm not praying. I'm getting out of this war. I'm going back to Blighty...

TAFFY: But you're not due for any leave, and you haven't been wounded.

RON: No! But I'm master of my own destiny, boyo.

TAFFY: What do you mean?

RON: All I have to do is make sure I get wounded.

TAFFY: You could get killed, not wounded...

RON: Look, mate, I've a plan see. If I light a fag and put my right hand just over the top of the trench, some Bosch sniper is going to aim... and get me.

TAFFY: But you couldn't work after the war, Ron, you'd be a cripple. Maimed for life.

RON: I'd be alive, Taffy. Alive! Next time our officers send us over the top, I could be dead. (*He opens his tin*) The only things not damp in this muddy pisshole are my fags. (*He gets one out of his tin*)

TAFFY: Don't do it, Ron, not your right hand...and you've told me, Ron! You've told me and I could tell the sarge you did it on purpose...

RON: But you won't, will you, Taffy? We are mates...

TAFFY: (*Pausing*) No... I won't...we're mates...

RON: (*Laughing*) Yes, we are mates now, Taffy boyo. I'm what's called ambidextrous. I can use my left hand just as well as my right hand. Anyway, it's got to be my right hand as it will look suspicious if it's my left, and they will have to declare me unfit for military service and give me a fucking pension. A war pension will keep me going... (*Ron mimes lighting a cigarette and then places his right hand on the top of the trench*)
Just watch, it won't take long for that Bosch sniper to get me... (*Silence...followed by a single shot*)
Aagh! Oh, he's got me! Bloody hell! (*Ron doubles up in pain*) I've lost some fingers. (*He shouts at Taffy*) Get the bloody orderlies... I'm wounded... (*He falls to the floor*) It's Blighty for me... Blighty, here I come...wounded...but alive... (*He cries with pain and relief*) (*Taffy runs to get help*)

The Summer Holiday Essay

Ray is eating a snack during the school break and trying to tell a friend about what happened on a beach in Portugal during their family holiday. (This scene is based on a newspaper article)

RAY: (*Eating a packet of crisps*) I know I don't look very happy, 'cos I'm not, see...last lesson it was English, wasn't it? It's Tuesday...yeah! I know you have maths, but I have English with Mr Harris, an' he says, "Right! It's the first week back after the holidays, so you have to write an essay on 'My Summer Holiday' and you've all got forty-five minutes from now...no talking...and think details...be descriptive." Well, I nearly panicked... No! It wasn't that...it's because we had a terrible time...no! It didn't rain all the time...we went to Portugal and rented a villa...that was nice, about a ten-minute walk to the beach... Dad said it was extra expensive 'cos it was so close to the sea...but Mum wanted a beach holiday and she always wins.

Well, the first day we all went down to the beach. Mum made us all put our sunscreen on, factor 50...yeah! We needed it in Portugal. We settle down...the sun is really hot and the sea is blue and Mum says, "This is the life for me." Then she sees it...at the water's edge, just lying there motionless...an' all these Portuguese families are just sunbathing, running in an' out of the water, laughing, eating... enjoying themselves...ignoring what is lying there, Colin.

Mum says to Dad, "What's that over there by the water's edge?" and she gets up, walks over, and it's a body, a dead man...an' Mum gets hysterical an' Dad goes an' tries to calm her down, but he can't... she tells him to go an' find a lifeguard or policeman or something or someone...all these Portuguese families are just sitting there an' watching, not moving an' probably thinking she's some hysterical English woman.

Well… Dad runs off to find someone who can deal with dead bodies on the beach… I go with him 'cos I don't want to look at the body. Eventually, we find this policeman on the promenade and Dad says, "Hola, do you speak English?" And this guy says he can, so Dad tells him what we've seen…an' we are gobsmacked by what this policeman says: "Calm down, it's only a dead Somali. They try to come as migrants, they want to get smuggled in…but sometimes there are hundreds of them piled into an unsafe boat, it capsizes an' they all drown off our coastline…so the bodies get washed up all the time…it's nothing to get upset about…they are *illegal* migrants… it's a real problem…sometimes it's several bodies…someone will eventually come an' take the body away…just forget it…" And he shrugged like they all do in Portugal…

That's what this policeman said: "Forget it." When we went back, Mum was still crying…she'd packed everything up. She said we couldn't stay on that beach any longer, an' he was a young Somali, so we all went back to the villa…it really spoiled our holiday. That night, I couldn't sleep 'cos I just had this image of that poor man just washed up, dead. An' all he wanted was a better life in Europe. Mum and Dad said perhaps Weymouth would have been better… less traumatic…an' I really didn't want to write about it, not really, 'cos I'm still having nightmares about it… I wake up in a sweat with this terrible picture in my mind… I shouldn't have gone to look… it's gonna stay with me for the rest of my life.

So, in the end, with everyone writing madly all around me, I wrote this fantasy essay about staying with Gran in Weymouth and it rained nearly every day an' we didn't do much…what? Mr Harris might know the weather was great! Well, not in Weymouth an' if he says anything, I'll say where my gran lives has its own microclimate…and basically… I wish we had gone to Weymouth…

Art Class Chat

This scene is set in an art class. The actor mimes drawing a still life picture while talking to a fellow pupil. Aim to explore mime opportunities as the scene develops and the drawing is completed.

Viv: (*Holding a board with drawing paper pinned to it, and with various coloured pencils in front of her to choose from*) Miss brings in the most God-awful pots for us to draw. She says this is her "Moorcroft vase" as if it's worth thousands of pounds…well, yeah…it could be… but if it is, I don't think she'd bring it in…would she? And what did she say those flowers are she's stuck inside it…what? You're clever…aquilegia…they're not easy to draw, all itsy-bitsy with tiny leaves… I would rather draw roses, they're easy…and then she puts a pomegranate at the base of that vase and says it's there to "compliment the overall composition". I sometimes wonder what she's on… (*Viv concentrates on drawing*) What was your Sunday like? (*Viv concentrates on the drawing*) Boring! Don't you ever go anywhere? Yeah! I know being dragged round Tesco's isn't much fun 'cos your mum says it's quieter than Saturday. (*Starts to rub out some of the drawing*) Well…we had a mini-drama…mind… I don't think Mum would call it 'mini'…my mum does all the gardening as Dad is a full-time couch potato…yeah! He says he works too hard in the week to come an' slave away in our garden…says he needs his "chill-out" time…well, don't we all…that pomegranate is so hard to draw. (*Concentrating on it*) I wish Miss had just put a lemon there… I can draw lemons easily… (*Holds up the board to look at it*) You know this is the time the leaves fall off the trees…yeah! Autumn… Miss will be having us do leaf transfers next lesson…anyway… Mum gets into a real state about the leaves in the garden and our dog tracking them into the house, so she decided to sweep them all up…she took

the wheelie bin round the back…started to sweep up the leaves…
but there were masses of them…masses… Dad and me were out of
it watching the game on TV… Eventually, Mum had the wheelie
bin filled to the top, but she still has this big mound of leaves and
is on a mission to get rid of them…so, she decided to trample them
down in the bin…yeah! Well, you know my mum is about four foot
eight and fifteen stone, right! So…when she climbed into the bin
using the wheel to haul herself in…she squashed the leaves down
to nothing…like a foot…an' was then wedged down inside and
couldn't get out…just stuck inside the wheelie bin…yeah! I know it
was a crazy thing to do…she acts on impulse sometimes, like I do…
Well, we heard the dog barking his head off, but Dalmatians can do
that 'cos they're a bit neurotic, so we didn't pay any attention 'cos we
thought Mum was playing a ball game with him…but, in fact, she's
shouting her head off at the bottom of the garden… Dad and me
are engrossed in watching the game and can't hear her…yeah! And
she's sobbing in the wheelie bin 'cos it's like a nightmare…until,
finally, Reggie next door sees her from his bedroom window…belts
round, rings the doorbell and tells Dad that Mum is stuck in our
wheelie bin and can't get out… Dad thinks it's a big joke at first,
but then he starts to hear her. He goes round the back an' when
he sees her, he starts killing himself laughing…so, Mum gets a bit
more hysterical…an' me, Dad an' Reggie have to push the wheelie
bin onto its side to drag her out…an' Mum says she's not doing that
again… Dad says it was "stupid" anyway, which made her super
mad…she stomped upstairs an' went to bed… Dad an' me went
back to watching the game…an' she didn't make us any tea…look!
(*Holding up the drawing board to show the drawing to the other pupil*)
Do you think Miss will like my aquilegia?

A Rule is a Rule

The scene opens as Nicole Fisher, a girl about to take her GCSE exams, tells her mother about what has happened in school that day. Nicole enters the kitchen in a furious mood and throws her school bag on the floor. At first, her mother does not seem interested, but Nicole makes her mother listen to her. In the scene, Nicole's body language is an important element that supports what has happened in school and how she feels. Eyeline should be focussed on the unseen mother.

NICOLE: (*Throwing her school bag down*) That's it! I'm never going back! I'm done with school… OK, so I start my exams in three weeks' time… Mum! Will you stop what you are doing and look at me… Just look, will you? (*She stands defiantly in front of her mother*) Can't you see what they've done to me? (*The mother appears not to see*) Look! (*Nicole puts her hands up to her ears*) Plasters! Can't you see what they've made me do? My tutor didn't say anything; my subject teachers didn't say anything and it was changeover bell this afternoon when down the corridor comes Dracula Lady Mrs Purvis…yeah! Purvis PE, and she looks at me when I go past with those beady bloodshot eyes of hers…then calls out, "Nicole Fisher, you have earrings in your ears! Earrings are forbidden in this school. Come here!" She's got a voice like a foghorn…everyone swings round to look at me, her victim… Well, I just stand there…she crosses her arms like this… (*shows her mother*)…and she comes so close to me her spit is flicked in my face, ugh! "Take those earrings out!" And her voice is the one she uses on the hockey pitch, deafening, but she's right next to me. I say, "But Miss, I've just had my ears pierced for my sixteenth birthday and these are the sleepers and we have study leave at the end of next week," and I smile sweetly at her. But she says, "Don't smirk at me! There are rules in this school." A smile doesn't work on Mrs Purvis, so I try to explain that if I take the sleepers out, the holes will heal up and I won't be able to wear earrings. But she shouts, "Don't argue with me! A rule is a rule!" Then I thought I'd try crying, but remembered crying doesn't work on Mrs Purvis… I've tried that before and it doesn't work…so she says, "Come to the PE office with me. As you're being so stubborn, we will have to settle this another way." So, off we both go to the PE office…she rummages round her drawer until she finds some plasters… I'm not too pleased about this and she says, "You can take that sullen look off your face, Nicole. This is a health and safety issue." And I can't get my head around that we are just dealing with the sleepers in my earlobes! She makes me put these plasters over my sleepers…when I finally get to my English lesson, I could see Cathy and Pearl sniggering away…

Then, at the end of school, who should be on bus duty but Mrs Purvis. I walk past with my plasters and I could see her sniggering as she told Miss Wills about me. So, that winds me up. When I get to the top of the driveway, Mrs Purvis shouts out in her foghorn voice, "Nicole Fisher! That skirt of yours is too short! Make sure it is the regulation length by tomorrow morning." So, I turn around and shout back, "Is it a health and safety risk, Miss?" Then she goes bananas and screams, "Tomorrow, you've got a detention after school in the PE office, for being rude! Make sure you're there!"

But Mum, I'm not going back… I've had it with school… Mum! Don't look like that… I mean it…this time, I mean it…

The Dinner Queue

The scene is set in a school dining hall. The actor should make sure that all the action is played out towards the audience. The dinner queue should be staged in such a way that Chuckie is able to speak to the kitchen staff facing directly outwards so that facial play can add its own supportive dimension to any mimed action.

CHUCKIE: (*Being pushed and turning to the dinner queue*) Hey! Will you lot stop pushing...just calm down, will ya! There's enough food for everyone...just wait your turn. (*Speaking to his friend*) It's that big fat lump Elliott what's pushing... I hate being in front of him... He just pushed his way in an' Sir is never around to send him to the back of the queue. I thought the rule was, if you pushed in you got sent to the back, but I dunno, there are no rules for some an' rules for others. Now, if I pushed in, Sir would get me! Oh yes! If I pushed in, he'd come down on me like a ton of bricks...but not for fat boy Elliott... Sir never seems to be looking when he does it... OK, I shouldn't call him fat...he didn't hear me anyway, he's too busy pushing everybody. (*There's another big push*) Will you stop pushing! (*Looks at menu on wall*) So, what's on the menu today? Vegetarian pasty! Yuk! They're all mushy and tasteless and full of tomatoes, yuk! (*Reads again*) Jacket potatoes with baked beans! Oh no, don't sit next to Gary or Sam this afternoon. (*Waves hand past his nose*) It will be smelly, like really whiffy... (*Looking at menu again*) Oh good, spaghetti bolognaise please...yeah! I'm starving...thanks, great! That's an enormous dollop of sauce...yumeee... (*Turning to his friend*) Yuk! You're not having the vegetarian pasty are you...you must have a cast iron stomach...you should have looked at the vegan menu...right, come on...let's get that table over there before Elliott comes along. (*Moves off with friend and mimes picking up cutlery on the way*) Yuk! These forks are revolting…you'd never guess they've been put through a dishwasher. (*Shows a fork to his friend*) Look at this one. Disgusting! It looks as if it's covered in egg yolk… I'm not having this… (*Picks up a knife*) Look at this knife…it's bent! (*Finally chooses a knife and fork*) Come on, let's grab that table. (*Runs over*) I hate being the last group into dinner…look at the state of this table…squashed baked beans everywhere…it's year 11… I hate year 11, they think they can do what they like 'cos they go on study leave at the end of the week…a fine lot of 'studying' that lot will do… I heard Sir say it's because they nearly all "belong to the Chinese zodiac year of the tiger and they're all cats"! That doesn't sound too good to me. (*Eating*) I'd like to know what Chinese sign of the zodiac I am… (*Eating*) What's your vegetarian pasty like? You could try the vegan option tomorrow…but I won't… I don't like the sound of vegan…it sounds tasteless… Oh, you like your pasty? Well, lucky you…

Modern Manners:
A Sixth Form Induction Day

The scene is set in a sixth form centre where an invited speaker is giving an etiquette demonstration to the students. It's the start of lower sixth form and the students have already had problem-solving and bonding activities in the morning session. The speaker is enthusiastic about sharing dinner table etiquette and constantly interacts with the students in a light-hearted manner. Eye focus suggests a group of listeners in a semicircle. On a table in front of the speaker is a set of cutlery. There is also a mobile phone.

SPEAKER: Right, you guys! Settle down…that's it. (*Looks around*) I hope you are all suitably hydrated after those problem-solving activities on the playing fields. (*Smiles*) Very challenging…it looked like more chiefs than Indians to me. (*The students don't respond to this*) OK! So, what is this session all about? (*Smiles*) "Modern manners at the dinner table." (*Laughs*) Mind you, some of these rules are left over from Victorian times. It was the Victorians who refined the way we eat… (*Someone interrupts*) Yes? No! Not "grab a hamburger to go" but to sit down and be civilised and to converse with each other… (*Holding up the mobile phone*) And this is absolutely forbidden at the dinner table… (*Holding a hand in admonishment*) I know this means cut off from your friends for three to four hours, but if you are invited out to dinner you are there to talk to the other guests…not on your mobile phone… (*There is obvious consternation from the listeners*) I know this is a hard rule to follow. (*Someone interrupts*) No! Emergency calls will have to wait… A suicidal friend? (*Exasperated*) Then your friend will have to move on and call another friend… Look! It's most unlikely you are the only friend… No! You cannot leave the dinner table to take the call outside! Calm down, everyone… Right!

Let's move on. (*Holding some cutlery*) Now, you've all been given a set of cutlery. Place on the table in front of you a place setting for a dinner guest. (*Watches this done*) Ah! (*Lifting up a demonstration knife*) I see that some of you have placed the cutting edge of the knife outwards. That is wrong. A knife should face inward with the edge towards the plate. And I also see that some of you have put your pudding spoon and fork along the top of the setting. That is a hotel setting. At home, the fork and spoon are placed at the side... (*Looking around*) I see some of you don't agree. I'm just telling you what is correct...and there should never be more than five pieces of cutlery for each dinner guest. (*Holding them up*) A soup spoon, main course knife and fork, pudding spoon and fork...if you need a cheese knife, that can be put on the table later... OK, pudding sounds babyish. If you want to say dessert spoon, that's fine... Ah! Good! You've got a question. (*Listens as the question is asked*) Right...so the question is, "What do you do if you've got something in your mouth that you want to spit out?" Well, what you must never ever do is spit something out... No! Not in your serviette...it's called a napkin, by the way... Right! Good question...if it's a fish bone...good suggestion. (*Smiles at the student*) The rule is that you put it on the piece of cutlery you used to put it in your mouth... (*Picks up a demonstration fork*) So...you would be eating the fish like this (*demonstrates*) and you put the bone neatly on the back of the fork where it's not going to fall through the tines...easy...and if you want to get rid of a cherry stone... (*Picks up a spoon*) Pop it onto the spoon... No! You don't turn the spoon upside down, don't be silly... (*Puts the spoon down*) Now, let's consider the really challenging part of the dinner...cutting the cheese the right way. Here we have very simple guidelines... Yes! (*Nodding to a student*) Even the queen follows the rules... OK, you guys. (*Smiling at some who have interrupted*) Perhaps Prince Harry doesn't, but I assure you the rest of the royal family know how to cut cheese correctly...if it's a round cheese, like a whole Camembert, you cut it like a cake, so it's wedge-shaped...if it's a big wedge of soft French cheese you cut it along the side at an angle, not straight across...the French call that 'cutting the nose off' the cheese and it is considered a dinner table crime. Now, if you are passed a cheeseboard with English cheese… (*Suddenly a bell rings*) Oh! There's the bell…and I wanted to tell you about Wensleydale… Please guys…as you leave take an evaluation sheet and fill it in… (*Calling out*) Hand it to your tutors…hope you enjoyed the presentation…remember that old saying: "Manners maketh man."

At the Art Gallery: A School Trip

A school group is at the National Gallery to look at specific paintings. Their task is to 'read them'. In this scene, two pupils are looking at Jan Van Eyck's The Arnolfini Marriage. They carry clipboards with worksheets and pens to record their observations. This scene is presented looking outwards to the audience so that all facial play and movements can be clearly seen. It is an exercise in not seeing the audience, but focussing on the imagined painting hanging on a wall in front of them.

TUBS: This has got to be it. Gallery 22. (*Pointing*)

JAY: These are really small. I like big pictures. The bigger the better.

TUBS: It's all about spatial awareness, Jay.

JAY: What does that mean?

TUBS: Don't you remember, Jay? Sir said in class, "Size matters and how we relate to the image…"

JAY: Yeah…

TUBS: With a big picture, you stand well back and it's a vista…or it can be panoramic…

JAY: Well, these are tiny…

TUBS: So, we go right up and have an intimate connection with them… sometimes it's like looking through a keyhole. (*Peering forward at the image*)

JAY: Yeah! I remember thinking it sounded silly…

TUBS: Come on, let's get up close…but not too close…

(*They move forward and start peering at the imagined painting*)

JAY: The Arnolfini Marriage, 1454.

TUBS: It's great, isn't it? And not too small…

JAY: How can it be a marriage when they aren't even in church? It looks like a bedroom…

TUBS: Sir said they didn't have to go to church to get married in 1454.

And rich people had beds everywhere…

JAY: They don't look very happy. In fact, she looks miserable…

TUBS: It's because it's a solemn occasion. It isn't a 'laugh a minute jokey situation' when you get married…

JAY: I think he's ugly…

TUBS: He's a rich Italian merchant living in Bruges…

JAY: So, she's onto a winner then? Forget the face…

TUBS: She's rich too. Look at her clothes.

JAY: There's a lot of dress…yards and yards of it. It's a pity she's pregnant…

TUBS: No, she isn't! Sir said the rich had more cloth in their clothes than they needed as a sign of wealth. Conspicuous consumption. She has just piled up the folds of her dress onto her stomach.

JAY: So, it's a statement she's got pots of money…

(They pause to look at the painting)

TUBS: I like the symbolism of the dog at her feet…

JAY: It looks like a Yorkshire terrier to me…

TUBS: A Yorkie in Bruges! No, it's a Belgian breed, probably a rat catcher. It symbolises fidelity and duty…

JAY: How do you know that?

TUBS: Sir gave us a lesson on symbols in painting. That dog is more than just a dog. You were ill…

JAY: OK. So, what does that orange mean on the windowsill?

TUBS: Sir said caring husbands gave their pregnant wives oranges and the segments and seeds are a sign of fertility…he wants her to have lots of babies…

JAY: So, she is pregnant!

TUBS: No! It's the dress and all that material…

JAY: Well, they got their vitamin C then…

TUBS: Yeah! But they didn't know about vitamin C in 1454…it's a symbol of his future hopes…

(They look at the painting and write down notes on their pads)

JAY: That's a funny-looking window, isn't it?

TUBS: It's because the only way to have glass windows was to use wine bottle bottoms…

JAY: So that's why it's all circles. They couldn't see out…

Tubs: No! But it let light in and kept the rain out. Only the rich had windows like that in 1454.

Jay: I'm glad I didn't live then…

Tubs: Sir said the point about this picture is it's a "time capsule – a specific moment that we can all relate to…" and also think about…

Jay: I'm not sure I'm relating to it…but I like the colours…the red bed is nice…and that mirror on the back wall is amazing…

(Jay steps a bit closer to peer at the painting)

Tubs: This picture has amazing perspective. You've just spotted one of its greatest features…

Jay: *(Turning to Tubs)* Really?

Tubs: Yes! That mirror! It reflects the interior of the room… Van Eyck has got it all in there in that mirror and if you look carefully, he's put himself in it with a priest standing beside him to bless the marriage.

(Jay looks again)

Jay: Yeah! He must be the guy in blue…and you can see…look, a rosary hanging on the wall…

(Jay points, but a supervisor calls out "Don't touch the painting" and Jay is startled)

… But I wasn't touching the painting. My finger was at least an inch away!

Tubs: They have eyes in the backs of their heads, these room supervisors…

Jay: I was inches away…really…

Tubs: They get nervous with school parties…all wound up…they think we don't know how to treat paintings…

Jay: Right! Have we finished with this one?

Tubs: *(Checking clipboard)* Yeah! Now we move on to the *Rout of San Romano* by Uccello, and it's a big one…

Jay: So, stand well back and treat it as a vista, eh?

Tubs: Or a panorama…come on…it's in the next gallery and my sheet says… *(looking at it)*…it's in tempera…

Jay: Whatever that means…

Tubs: Jay! It's on your worksheet…it tells you how the Italians used tempera…all you gotta do is read it…

(They move into the next room)

The Ecology Trip

Two pupils are on a day trip to the sea to study the ecology of the foreshore.
They carry clipboards with their worksheets attached. They also have plastic
buckets to collect the plastics they find along the beach. Both are very aware of
the world around them. Georgie uses an inhaler.

JAY: (*Out of breath*) Good. We've managed to get away from that lot…
    They are all fighting over the plastic bottles they find. And they all
    want to be winners…

GEORGIE: (*Panting*) Yes! We can share what we find fifty-fifty without
    arguing about who saw it first. That's a deal, isn't it, Jay?

JAY: Yes! Look… (*pointing*)…there's a plastic bottle and a plastic bag.

GEORGIE: Right. You have the bottle. I'll have the bag, and next time I'll
    have the bottle…

    (*They pick up these objects and put them into their buckets*)

JAY: (*Writing on a worksheet*) Found one Evian bottle…

GEORGIE: (*Writing on worksheet*) One large plastic bag… Do you know,
    Jay, that they find dolphins with their stomachs full of plastic bags?
    It's horrible… Hang on…here we are making a list of all the plastic
    thrown away on the beach and putting it into a plastic bucket…

JAY: Yeah! I don't think Sir thought that one through. We should have
    biodegradable bags…

GEORGIE: This sea air is bad for my asthma. (*Pulls out an inhaler and uses
    it*) Oh! That's better… I gotta be careful, Jay, my mum said sea air
    is too damp.

JAY: No, it isn't! Sea air is full of *ozone*…breathe it all in… (*Taking a deep
    breath*) And smell the salt in the air. I'm sure it's healthy. The
    Victorians loved ozone-filled sea air!

GEORGIE: (*Putting away the inhaler*) I am not a Victorian…all I can smell
    is this rotting seaweed…

JAY: We've got to take a sample. (*Stoops down to pick some seaweed*) There are lots of different kinds around here. We're spoiled for choice…

GEORGIE: Then you can have the sample in your bucket…

JAY: (*Pointing towards two deckchairs*) Look, Georgie! Two abandoned deckchairs.

GEORGIE: How do you know they're abandoned, Jay?

JAY: (*Exasperated*) Because there's no one sitting in them.

GEORGIE: But they could be swimming or paddling or gone to get an ice cream…

JAY: Can you see anyone swimming or paddling? There's no gear around the deckchairs. People would have stuff with them. Beach towels and stuff!

GEORGIE: We haven't got any stuff!

JAY: We've got clipboards and collection buckets…and we're on an ecology trip. Have you got anything ticked off your worksheet? It can be anything that isn't biodegradable…

GEORGIE: Yeah. Seaweed and a big plastic bag. I bet it had someone's picnic in it…

JAY: Remember, Georgie, seaweed is biodegradable… Look! There's definitely no one using those deckchairs. Come on! Let's sit in them…
(*They go over to the deckchairs and settle down*)

GEORGIE: (*Taking a tube of sunscreen out and starting to spread it over his face*) My mum said I've got to be very careful and not get sunburned.

JAY: Good idea.

GEORGIE: This is factor 50.

JAY: That sounds high?

GEORGIE: It's total blockage. Do you want some?

JAY: (*Taking the tube*) Might as well. (*Spreading it over his face*) I don't want to end up all red-faced. (*Hands the tube back to Georgie*)
(*They sit looking out to sea*)

GEORGIE: I'm going to take off my socks and shoes. (*Takes them off*)

JAY: Good idea. (*Does the same*) Hey, do you think you should put factor 50 on your feet? They look very white.

GEORGIE: Nah! I'm going to risk it…

JAY: Yeah! I'll do the same…

(They look around)

GEORGIE: From here, I can see at least three plastic bottles…really big ones. *(Pointing)* Over there…

JAY: And four plastic bags in with the seaweed…and a plastic bowl that must have fallen off a yacht.

GEORGIE: And look! *(Points in front)* That seagull is pecking a polystyrene plank or something. How are we going to get a polystyrene plank in our collection buckets? It's a really thick one…massive…

JAY: We'll jump on it, and have half each. Right? Fifty-fifty…

GEORGIE: My asthma is playing up. *(Gets out an inhaler)* I told you sea air isn't good for me…

JAY: *(Ignoring Georgie)* And I'll go and jump on that big bit of polystyrene. Plastic is going to destroy our planet. It's already ruined our beach here, and I bet polystyrene takes hundreds of thousands of years to biodegrade…

(Jay mimes jumping on the polystyrene and breaking it up)

GEORGIE: You're doing a great job, Jay, go at it…smash it up…

JAY: *(Miming)* Here's your bits and I've got mine… Sir is going to be well pleased with us… Polystyrene just reveals the whole ecological disaster on the seashore. Whoever invented it didn't do us any favours…

Seashore Detectives: A Field Trip

This scene takes place along a seashore. Pupils have come on a geography field trip to study and assess the ecology of the beach. They have clipboards with worksheets attached. They also have backpacks. It is a sandy shoreline with rocks and rock pools. This scene includes a lot of physicality, including mime sequences, which help to support the action. The pupils frequently refer to their teacher's notes on their clipboards.

SPINK: Now remember, Toni, Sir says we have to keep in mind that a beach is a living organism, and we must respect it…

TONI: I hate geography…

SPINK: No, you don't…

TONI: Yes, I do! And Sir is boring, always going on about fossils in rocks…

SPINK: Look. It's better than being stuck in school, in a hot classroom…

TONI: Well… I'm cold…really cold…

SPINK: Then you should have put three layers on, like me… Sir said, "Dress up warm."

TONI: (*Shrugs*) This sea air isn't good for my asthma…

SPINK: (*Ignoring Toni*) Come on…let's look for lugworms…

TONI: Lugworms? (*Grimaces*)

SPINK: (*Exasperated*) Yes! Look… (Pointing to worksheet) It says, "Lugworms live in U-shaped burrows on sandy beaches."

TONI: OK…which this is…and I've got sand in my trainers 'cos we had to come through those sand dunes…

SPINK: (*Ignoring Toni and reading from the sheet*) "And lugworms swallow and eat any pieces of food they find in it." Now, that's good for the ecology…

TONI: Ugh! Spink, it says, "The sand comes out of the worm's bottom at the other end of their burrow, and makes a squiggly worm cast on the surface of the sand."

SPINK: Right! So, let's look for squiggly things. (*They both look around*)

TONI: Found some! (*Pointing*) Nearly stepped on it...so that's my first tick of the day.

SPINK: Yeah! OK... (*Ticks sheet*) Now... Sir says there is usually a pile of washed-up seaweed and other debris at the high-water mark...

TONI: Spink...it's 'debree', that word. (*Leaning over, pointing at Spink's worksheet*) It's pronounced 'debree'...the s is silent...

SPINK: How do you know, smarty-pants?

TONI: Because Sir said it in class when he was talking us through the worksheet...

SPINK: Know it all!

TONI: I just pay attention...

SPINK: Even if you "hate geography"?

TONI: Oh, shut up, Spink. You don't like me knowing something you don't know. Let's look at our sheets. (Looking at clipboard) Sir has written, "The high-water mark is called the strandline. Here you will find lots of dried seaweed, egg cases of whelks, the empty egg cases of dogfish, called mermaid's purse, cuttlefish bones, crab claws and lots of shells."

SPINK: Good! That sounds as if it will give us lots of ticks...

TONI: And listen! "And birds search the strandline for small animals to eat..."

SPINK: Right then! (*They move forward*) Look! There's lots of dried-up seaweed over there. (*Pointing*) So, it must be the strandline...
(*They both move over to an imagined strandline at the front of the performance space*)

TONI: Ugh! I think seaweed smells...

SPINK: (*Delighted*) Look, Toni! Bladderwrack seaweed. (*Shows Toni the worksheet*) It's just like Sir's picture...

TONI: It doesn't look dried out to me...

SPINK: That's because it's bladderwrack seaweed!

TONI: Does that mean a tick?

SPINK: Yes! (*Pointing to worksheet*) It says, "Bladderwrack seaweed has pockets of air and jelly to help it stay afloat in the water. Its tough, leathery leaves are covered in a slippery, gummy substance to protect it from drying out at low tide…"

TONI: OK! So, bladderwrack can survive out of water while the tide is out…we're finding out a lot about seaweed…

SPINK: And look! (Bending down) These must be cuttlefish bones. All we need now are crab claws. (Picks up the cuttlefish and examines it)

TONI: Put it back, Spink. Sir says we have to protect and preserve the ecology an' not take anything away…

SPINK: Come on, Toni, let's sit down here and look out to sea…

TONI: It's a bit damp…

(They settle down and look outwards)

SPINK: Sir said we might see dolphins and seals.

TONI: (Reading) "And when sea otters in the northwest Pacific Ocean sleep, they wrap themselves in giant sea kelp seaweed to anchor themselves down…"

SPINK: Seaweed is amazing, isn't it, Toni? The Welsh eat the stuff…

(They look outwards and then jump up and start pointing and shouting in unison)

TONI: Look! A seal…

SPINK: No! It's a dolphin…

TONI: Sir! It's a seal…

SPINK: Sir! It's a dolphin…

TOGETHER: Look! Look! Sir! And Miss! Out there…

Castle Detectives

Two pupils are on a fact-finding history trip to a medieval castle. The aim is to learn about the way the building was planned. They have backpacks and clipboards with worksheets. The castle overlooks the sea, and the scene includes a lot of physicality, including mime sequences that help support the dialogue. They regularly refer to their clipboard information sheets.

SAM: Hey, Ollie! This is interesting. It says, "2000 castles were built in Great Britain between 1066 and 1485…"

OLLIE: I hate learning dates.

SAM: OK. But it's interesting, isn't it?

OLLIE: I hope Sir doesn't expect us to visit them all.

SAM: No. They'll be spread out geographically, won't they? Not an hour away like this one.

OLLIE: Let's stay in this doorway so those seagulls can't get us. I hate seagulls.

SAM: This isn't just a doorway, Ollie. This is a gatehouse, and look… (*Pointing upwards*) Those are murder holes used for dropping things on attackers.

OLLIE: Such as?

SAM: Molten lead, red-hot cinders!

OLLIE: I bet that hurt.

SAM: And see that gap? That's where the portcullis came down to make it even harder for the attackers to get in.

OLLIE: It says here we have to find the sally port. (*Reading*)

SAM: Right. It will be a small postern door in a tower. Let's move.

OLLIE: But the seagulls will dive-bomb us.

SAM: You've got a thing about seagulls, haven't you?

OLLIE: Yeah! They drop 'things' on you. (*Makes a grimace*)

SAM: Stop being a wimp. Come on. We've got to go on a search, as the sally port was used to make raids on the enemy. So, it's got to be at the base of a tower.

(*They leave the gatehouse area*)

OLLIE: Look over there. Is that a sally port? (*Pointing*)

SAM: No! It's the entrance to a donjon.

OLLIE: A what?

SAM: A donjon. That's Norman French for a dungeon. This is a Norman castle.

(*They approach an opening*)

OLLIE: It looks like a nasty hole to me.

SAM: It's supposed to be nasty! You don't want prisoners to enjoy themselves. Come on, let's go down these steps.

OLLIE: You go down. I don't like the look of it. It looks like a 'health and safety' risk. Sir said we are not to do anything risky.

SAM: Yes! Like go up on the battlements. But this is going down.

OLLIE: We can still fall. Like fall down the steps rather than off the battlements. I am not going down.

SAM: OK... (*Looking at sheet on clipboard*) We are supposed to sketch the plan of the motte and bailey.

OLLIE: Is motte Norman French for moat?

SAM: No! It's Norman French for mound. (*Pointing*) Like that mound the keep is on. This is all the bailey. Where things happened. (*Sweeping arms around in a grand gesture*)

OLLIE: What sort of things?

SAM: (*Exasperated*) Were you switched off or something when Sir told us?

OLLIE: You know I've been off school. I missed that preparation lesson.

SAM: OK, OK. In this part... (*he gesticulates*)...all around here there would be...like wooden buildings...and stuff...

OLLIE: What sort of stuff?

SAM: All sorts of stuff. (*Exasperated*) Look, ask Sir when you see him. Right!

OLLIE: There's no need to get wound up 'cos I'm asking questions. You seem to know a lot...

SAM: Look! There's the chapel...all castles had their own chapel 'cos they were really religious. Come on, let's go and take a look. (*Marching off*)

OLLIE: (*Following*) Yeah! An' I bet there's a lot to discover...an' a lot to write down. (*Suddenly stopping*) Oh! No! It says, "Make a sketch of both the exterior and interior of the 1109 chapel, which is a remarkable Norman gem." Sam! Wait! Can you help me draw the chapel? I need your help, like, big time...

The Dream Pillow

Debbi is a teenage girl with Asperger's syndrome who is homeschooled. As the scene opens, she is sitting at home, concentrating on writing in a notebook. However, during the scene she is distracted by the noise of her mother putting out the household rubbish. Hearing a noise, she goes to look out the window and sees her mother placing her pillow beside the dustbin ready to be taken to the recycling plant.

DEBBI: (*Writing down carefully*) Henry VIII ordered a sword to cut off Anne Boleyn's head…a fine sword…a fine French sword…this was a massive kingly favour…all the other people had their heads chopped off with an axe…a horrid English axe…a blunt axe…but Anne was given specialist treatment…a very sharp sword. (*She is distracted by a noise outside, and goes to the window; she sees her pillow being thrown out*) My pillow! Why is my pillow outside? My pillow is my special night-time friend… Mummy has thrown away my special friend who keeps me safe at night… Mummy!
(*She leaves the room in a hurry and runs outside*)
Mummy! Mummy, what are you doing with my friend? (*She picks up the pillow*) I love my friend…my dream-maker friend! She lives inside my pillow and sends wonderful dreams into my head…why do you want to throw my friend away? I love my friend. (*Debbi starts to cry*) She's small and cute and cuddly. (*She cuddles her pillow*) OK! So, I spilled coffee on my dream pillow and it's soaked through… I don't care… I like it with coffee stains and I don't want it sent to the dump…it's too special for that…
(*Debbi runs further away from her mother, clutching the pillow*)
I love my pillow. (*She begins to kiss it*) Lovely, cuddly pillow…and inside is my lovely cuddly dream-maker friend… (*She stops and looks vehemently at her mother*) Yes! Deep, deep, deep inside…and her

name...is... Anushka...'cos she's Russian...a Russian dream-maker who gives me lovely dreams about snow princesses...and Russian bears and wolves too...and all night long, I am in Anushka's magical snow world...all sparkly...the bears come and dance for me...like this... (*Debbi starts to dance freely with her pillow*) But they can't do a *pirouette* like this... (*she demonstrates*)...or a *plié* like this... (*demonstrates*)...and definitely not a *jeté*... (*she demonstrates again*)...because, although they are Russian, they do not belong to a corps de ballet... (*She laughs*) And they absolutely refuse to wear tutus! They are just big white, furry, fluffy bears that dance around like this... (*Again, Debbi moves around in a lively free-flowing dance*) Then Anushka and the bears all give me kisses, lovely big kisses... lovely big smackers on the lips... I love that... I love them... I love my pillow...it's my dream-pillow...mine...mine... (*She runs into a corner, clutching her pillow*)

(*Debbi sits on the floor and covers the pillow with her body*)

It is MINE! And I will never ever give it up to be thrown out. NEVER!

(*Debbi caresses and kisses her pillow while looking defiantly at her mother*)

This pillow is never ever going to the DUMP! Ever!

Washed Ashore

Bodie is telling a friend about a summer trip to Cornwall and what he saw washed ashore on the beach at Hayle. (Based on a newspaper article)

BODIE: OK, so you went to Alicante, but I bet you didn't see what Dad and me saw on the beach at Hayle...that's in Cornwall. OK, so it's not known for baking hot summer days...but you get a lot of surfers there... Look...you can tell me about Alicante after I tell you what we saw, yeah... Me and Dad were walking along the beach when we saw all these surfers standing around something on the sand... yeah...right at the water's edge. So, Dad says, "Come on, let's go and see." Well, I was hoping it wasn't a body...you know...someone who had got drowned or fallen off a cliff...are you listening to me?... Well, turn your mobile off then... So, Dad says it looks like a massive dolphin...yeah...and we'd seen dolphins the day before... and I wasn't happy about seeing a dead one 'cos they're cute, aren't they? Like people save up tons of money to go swimming with the dolphins in the Caribbean, don't they? Anyway, when we get there, it isn't a dolphin...it's a shark...and this lifeguard Marine Trust man is all excited and saying to the surfers that it's not one of those dangerous sharks like Jaws...but...now...what did he call it? Ah!... Yes, a thresher shark and he said they only have a small mouth, so if one did go for you, it would only take a small lump out of your leg... but that could put you off surfing for life, couldn't it? This man from the Marine Trust measured it up and it was twelve feet long and he says, "You know, these can grow up to twenty feet long." And I think, does that mean a bigger mouth, a bigger bite? 'Cos if it does, I'm never going surfing off the Cornish coast...perhaps those weren't dolphins we saw...but sharks!

Anyway, one of the lifeguards who was helping to measure up this shark says, "Hey, we could start up a new business shark hunting out of Hayle harbour," and he gets his mates quite excited and they're thinking they could make a mint of money in the summer season... but I think swimming with the dolphins would be nicer... OK...so the water is freezing cold in Cornwall... Will you turn that mobile off! Have you been listening to me?

The Fishing Trip

The scene is set alongside the banks of a river where two friends are looking for a good place to fish. They carry their fishing rods and tackle.

TONI: The last time I came along here was with my dad. We caught a trout that big. (*Showing his friend an incredibly big size*)

SMITHY: You've got to be kidding! Trout don't grow that size.

TONI: Yes, they do…in this river.

SMITHY: Well, think again. Perhaps your memory is a bit faulty.

TONI: No, it isn't!

SMITHY: (*Stopping*) Look, Toni, it couldn't have been that big. (He tries to replicate what Toni has shown)

TONI: I didn't say he was that big! (*Shows a smaller fish*)

SMITHY: That's smaller than the first one!

TONI: No, it isn't!

SMITHY: Yes, it is! First of all, you said this size… (*Shows Toni again*) But now you've reduced it to this size… (*Changing the size to a smaller fish*)

TONI: OK! OK! It's not worth arguing over. Let's just say it was a big 'un and it was delicious…

SMITHY: Well, it would be, wouldn't it? (*Sarcastically*)

TONI: What do you mean by that?

SMITHY: What do you mean, "What do you mean by that"? I don't mean anything…

TONI: You sounded sarcastic.

SMITHY: Sorry! Didn't mean to.

TONI: Let's get a move on and find a good pitch…

SMITHY: We won't catch anything at this rate.

(*They move on a little*)

TONI: My dad says pitch up opposite the willow tree.

SMITHY: Which tree?

Toni: The willow tree…he says it's the best part of the river. He always catches something there.

Smithy: Yeah! A big fish this size… (*He mimes the same big size shown to him earlier*)

Toni: Are you taking the mick or something?

Smithy: No. (Shrugging) You're being touchy…

Toni: My dad is the best angler in the fishing club…he always catches something.

Smithy: Well, my dad only catches flies with his mouth wide open when he snores his head off on the sofa.

Toni: I know I shouldn't say it, but he sounds like a couch potato.

Smithy: But you just said it!

Toni: No, I didn't! I said, "I know I shouldn't say it."

Smithy: Look, I agree with you. Even my mum says he ought to "get up off that sofa and find something to do". But he never shifts…

Toni: My mum says my dad is hyperactive 'cos he's always doing something. I think she'd like him to sit on the sofa and be with her.

Smithy: Dad says he's dead beat after a day at work.

Toni: Look! (*Pointing across the river*) There's the willow tree.

Smithy: How do you know it's a willow tree, Toni?

Toni: 'Cos my dad described it to me.

Smithy: Your dad knows a lot. It looks just like a tree to me.

Toni: My dad is good at everything, an' he knows his trees…his favourite is a maple.

Smithy: My dad is good at snoring! All trees are just trees to him…
(*They get settled on the riverbank and mime getting their fishing gear ready*)

Toni: (*Throwing a line out*) Right! Here goes. Let's see if the fish are nibbling today.

Smithy: (*Throwing a line out*) It's a challenge…let's see who gets the first fish.

Toni: Seeing that notice over there reminds me… (*Points across the river*) You did get the day licences to fish here, didn't you?

Smithy: When was I supposed to do that?

Toni: Yesterday, you were supposed to go to the estate office and buy two one-day licences to fish along this river.

SMITHY: No! You said you'd get them.

TONI: No, I didn't!

SMITHY: Yes, you did!

TONI: When?

SMITHY: Yesterday!

TONI: (*Winding in the line*) Well, that's it. Fishing over.

SMITHY: Why? There's no one around...

TONI: Can't you read? It says it's a £100 fine if we are caught fishing without a licence.

SMITHY: (*Winding in his line*) So fish is off the menu, then.

TONI: (*Putting away his gear*) Yes! Whatever size...at the moment, it's no size.

(*They move away from the riverbank*)

I'm fed up! Really fed up!

SMITHY: With me?

TONI: I'm not going to say anything...just leave it...

The Tattoo

It is early in the morning, before college. The doorbell rings and Claire goes to see who's there. On the doorstep, she finds Susy, holding a bag of clothes. Susy has left home after an argument with her father, who has discovered that she has a tattoo. She has decided to go to her friend Claire's house until her father cools down.

CLAIRE: (*Opening door*) This is a bit early for you. What's up?

SUSY: (*Angrily going in*) Dad and me had a bust-up last night. He's been on a nerd-rant, with me as his victim.

CLAIRE: God! You're in a strop…

SUSY: Yeah! An' I'm not going back. (*She dumps her bag down*) He's done it this time. He's a weirdo an' I've had enough. He's like some old fogey living in the 1940s.

CLAIRE: Your dad's not that old.

SUSY: He acts as if he is. I've had it this time. I am not going back. Why do I have to end up with a dad who's bloody-minded an' awkward?

CLAIRE: I've always liked your dad. He's easier to get on with than mine.

SUSY: OK. Let's do a swap!

CLAIRE: It's not as easy as that, is it? Now, calm down, Susy, and tell me what's got you going this time…

SUSY: It was last night. We're all sitting there having our dinner an' my sister says to Dad, "Susy got a tattoo all up her arm." And Dad acts like a nutter, he nearly chokes on his chicken nuggets and says, "I told you, if you loved me, you wouldn't get a tattoo."

CLAIRE: Why has he got it in for tattoos?

SUSY: 'Cos his dad was an officer in the Royal Navy and officers never got tattoos.

CLAIRE: Is that true?

SUSY: I dunno. That's what he says…

CLAIRE: Some must have…

SUSY: Yeah! An' Dad says his dad said, "Only lower ranks get tattoos." Whatever that means. That's why he's been dead against me having one…

CLAIRE: It's a bit old-fashioned. Even celebrities like the Beckhams have tattoos…

SUSY: You're dead right! So, what's the big deal?

CLAIRE: So, you've left because he shouted at you?

SUSY: Claire, he went mental! I ran upstairs and locked myself in the bathroom. He was like a nutcase shouting at me. An' I thought he was goin' to hit me. So, I locked myself in the bathroom. It's the only room with a lock an' key.

CLAIRE: Did he carry on shouting?

SUSY: Shouting? He was so angry he beat the hell out of the door an' pushed the panels out…

CLAIRE: I would have been scared stiff.

SUSY: Mum was screaming at him…my sister was shouting her head off… an' the neighbours must have thought World War III had broken out.

CLAIRE: Were you shouting too?

SUSY: No! I was sitting on the loo cryin' my eyes out, wasn't I?

CLAIRE: So, what happened then?

SUSY: After he'd knocked the panels out, he stopped…

CLAIRE: He ran out of steam…

SUSY: He ran out of something…he'd probably hurt himself.

CLAIRE: I call that real anger, man, like mega angry!

SUSY: Yeah! Well, I sat there until it got quiet, then went to my bedroom and went to bed.

CLAIRE: Did he come in to shout at you again?

SUSY: No. The nutter didn't…

CLAIRE: I've always thought your dad is a chipper sort of guy, like, upbeat, definitely not a nutter.

SUSY: You don't have to live with him, do you?

CLAIRE: No! So, let's see your tattoo…

(*Susy rolls up her sleeve for Claire to see*)

SUSY: It's my sign of the zodiac, Pisces.

CLAIRE: (*Examining it*) It's a bit big. The fish curls all around your arm.

SUSY: Yeah! It's supposed to. I like it that way. (*She rolls her sleeve down again*) So, I left early this morning, out of my window, over the top of the garage, so Dad won't know. When I don't go down for college, he'll find my bed empty and me gone. He'll have a fit... serves him right...

CLAIRE: But he didn't hit you, did he?

SUSY: No! He just shouted his head off at me.

CLAIRE: Most dads shout around the place...mine does too.

SUSY: So, as he doesn't know where you live, can I stay here?

CLAIRE: That's difficult...

SUSY: Why?

CLAIRE: (*Putting her hands in the air and making speech mark movement*) Boring background alert! Mum and Dad think you're a bad influence on me...

SUSY: Me?

CLAIRE: Yeah! Welcome to my world, Susy.

SUSY: So, what am I expected to do?

CLAIRE: Go back home... (*She shrugs*) That's the best thing...

The Tour Guide

A group of visitors is assembled in the central hall of Pickersgill Manor. A young guide is attempting to get them to concentrate on the history of the manor and its contents.

GUIDE: Welcome to Pickersgill Manor, where the Pickersgills of Pickersgill have lived for over 400 years... (*Spotting some latecomers*) That's right...come in, we've only just started. Close the door please...the others are too late for our group and will have to wait... (*Turning back to the group*) Now, as you can see, this is the main hall where once all the banqueting happened... (*Breaking off*) Please! Please! (*Directing a gaze at a member of the group*) Don't touch the furniture...that is a sixteenth-century Dutch inlaid chest and your fingers will leave traces of acidity on the surface... (*Holding up bare hands*) We have to remember that ungloved fingertips can leave all sorts of acid marks that eat away at antique surfaces... (*Smiling in a patronising way*) If we can all look up for a minute at the rafters...yes! It will be "tough on the necks" as you say... (*Smiling in a patronising way at someone in the group*) But well worth it...as you see, the coat of arms of all the brides of the Pickersgills up to 1640...and clever children will spot them elsewhere on our tour... No! Madam! Don't sit on that sixteenth-century Jacobean chair...that's why it's got a teasel* on it... Please put the teasel back... I know it's easier to look up when one is sitting down, but the chairs are too valuable to be used... (*Smiles in a condescending manner and then moves to another position*) Now, the next really important feature is the fireplace... As you can all see... (*Breaks off and waves a hand*) Don't wander off... stay with our group in the centre hall please...this fireplace of local sandstone dates back to the 1590s... Shakespeare's time, children... (*Beams at the imagined children*) I am sure you are all studying one

94

of Shakespeare's plays in your English lessons... (*Imagine a child responding*) No? Well, you soon will be. The fireplace has biblical scenes taken from the Old Testament...can you all see Adam and Eve in the Garden of Eden...and Eve is tempting Adam with her apple... (*Irritated*) Yes! I know it looks like a pear, but I assure you it is an apple... Eve tempted Adam with the forbidden fruit... Yes! It could have been a pear but, in this carving, it is definitely an apple... (*Startled*) How do we know? (*Obviously annoyed*) Because this fireplace was originally painted in bright colours. The Elizabethans loved to use coloured paints wherever they could...and there are faint traces of colour if one looks closely... (*The guide moves in closer and points*) That forbidden fruit was once painted bright red. Apples are red, while pears are always painted yellow...that seems to confirm my opinion... Now, let's all move on together... (*The guide mimes opening a door*) No stragglers please...keep together... and I'll do a headcount as you pass through into the red dining room laid out for an Elizabethan feast... The centrepiece is that peacock... (*The guide mimes counting and calls out*) Children, look out for the coats of arms...there are five...don't touch! Remember the acidity in your fingers. Don't touch anything... (*Calling out*) And don't remove the teasels from the chairs...

*A teasel is a spiky dried flower head. Used by stately homes to prevent people sitting on chairs.

www.ingramcontent.com/pod-product-compliance
Lightning Source LLC
Chambersburg PA
CBHW021153090426
42740CB00008B/1076

JEFFREY GRENFELL-HILL trained for the professional theatre at the Bristol Old Vic Theatre School, where he was chosen as student director in his final year. After a tour of American colleges, universities and performing arts centres, he was invited to join the examining board of the London Academy of Music and Dramatic Art.

Jeffrey's poems have been included in Penguin and Heinemann anthologies, his plays have been published by Samuel French, and his monologues by Oberon Books in an anthology edited by Shaun McKenna. In 2019, Jeffrey published *Monologues and Duologues for Young Actors*, which offered drama teachers wider scene choice for the seven to thirteen age group. His popular monologues and duologues have been regularly chosen for the LAMDA examination acting syllabus as set pieces. They are often performed as 'own choice' selections at major festivals of speech and drama. Jeffrey himself is an adjudicator of many years' standing; this aspect of his career began when he was a member of the Board of Adjudicators at the Wyoming State Youth Drama Festival.

Jeffrey widened his career interests by reading history at Swansea University. This has inspired him to write more historical scenes; and has contributed to a belief in the complementarity of understanding history and drama. These scenes offer cross-curricular opportunities to teachers.

In 1994 Jeffrey was awarded a PhD in History by the University of Wales for work on the welfare of women and children in Wales from 1890 to 1930. He was also Director of Sixth Form Studies at St George's School, Harpenden, where he taught AS and A level Theatre Studies.

Jeffrey remains an examiner for the London Academy of Music and Dramatic Art and examines both in the United Kingdom and internationally.